Battleground

Peace Talks • Flak Attack • Ultimate Conflict

PRETEEN ELECTIVES
AGES 10-12

A Curriculum for Preteens

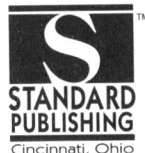

S™
STANDARD
PUBLISHING
Cincinnati. Ohio

Battleground

About the Authors

Churches, conventions, and seminars continue to seek *Linda Kondracki Sibley,* founder and executive director of Confident Kids, to train volunteers to minister to the needs of high-stress kids and families. Linda holds a master's degree in Christian education and pastoral care from Bethel Seminary and has fifteen years experience in church-related ministry to children and families. She is the author of the *Guides for Growing a Healthy Family* series published by Fleming H. Revell and a contributing editor for *Christian Parenting Today.*

Laurie Butts is an educator. She has served as a minister of Christian education, as well as a youth worker, Sunday school teacher, and curriculum writer. She has seven years of teaching experience in public schools.

Gail Maue has a bachelor's degree in deaf education. She received her masters in education for the hearing impaired from the University of Cincinnati. She has taught preteen Sunday school in the past and is currently a full-time middle school teacher.

Cover and inside illustrations by Scott Alan Roberts
Computer design by Peggy Theile

The Standard Publishing Company, Cincinnati, Ohio. A Division of Standex International Corporation. ©1997 The Standard Publishing Company

03 02 01 00 99 98 97   5 4 3 2 1
ISBN 0-7847-0647-6

Battleground

Beyond childhood, heading to the next level, preteens struggle with emotional and spiritual battles every day. Equip them to communicate clearly with family members. Guide them to resolve conflicts with others. Empower them to be on God's side in the war with Satan. Help them learn the secrets to winning in real life!

Why "Next Level"?

Upper elementary kids—we'll call them preteens—are reaching, striving, groping toward the next level. They're in transition. They want to be taller, stronger, faster, and smarter—as they catapult on their way to the next level.

In some ways preteens appear already to have arrived at the next level, (once termed junior high). Preteens want to wear the right clothes, match hairstyles with athletes or rock stars, and fit in with the peer group no matter what! For many, however, the next level is an elusive goal: manly muscles and feminine curves are controlled by hormones, not purchasing power.

So, too, the limits on thought structure. Many, if not most, fifth- and sixth-graders lack the ability to think critically, to form logical arguments, or draw general principles from specific examples. There is usually a wide gulf between their level of experience and their ability to reflect on the meaning of their experiences.

Preteens are also still resolving the issue: *What can I do well?* rather than tackling the adolescent question: *Who am I?* So when preteens dress and act like their peers they are striving for self-acceptance—feeling that they are as up-to-date as their peers, rather than establishing a personal identity. Erickson's studies show that ten to twelve year olds are less involved with establishing a personal identity than they are with figuring out what they're really good at. This disparity creates difficulties for those using junior high curriculum for preteen classes: What you see (a teenager) is not what you get (concrete-operational thinking and a different life task).

Next Level curriculum is transitional: to help transitional preteens feel comfortable in teen-style learning settings and to equip leaders to teach within the limits of preteen development. Lessons are structured to help you teach preteens effectively in groups. The younger the student, the more discussion guidance must be given to identify appropriate conclusions, and to suggest appropriate actions to be taken.

While many junior high topics are helpful and many elective curriculums look age appropriate, they often do not work with preteens because they were not designed for preteens' limited thought processing and inexperienced discussion skills.

Next Level Preteen Electives! Planned and designed with preteen issues in mind, and tailored for the learning capabilities of concrete thinkers! Visually appealing for the video generation. Emotionally satisfying for techno-driven kids.

This curriculum offers bonus opportunities for preteens to **Go to Extremes** serving others. It also strives to build family relationships—**Bridge the Gap**—during a fun-filled family session.

So, because life is not a game—
pick a topic and recruit some helpers.
Start a group for ten to twelve year olds—
They'll be glad you did!

Next Level Preteen Electives address the importance of instilling values for character development.

You can use **Next Level Preteen Electives** confidently, knowing that they are based on core biblical principles, permeated with Bible teaching, and presented in a way that ten to twelve year olds can understand and enjoy!

How are Next Level units organized?

Get Into the Game

As an introduction to the session, this section offers activities to grab the students' attention and encourages participation from the entire group.

These lesson steps offer activity choices that may be set up as learning centers or used as options. Depending on the class size, the teacher may divide the class into smaller groups to complete the activity. Each group works on the activity. For this to be effective, the teacher will need ample assistance.

If the class is small, the teacher can customize the session accordingly. Select one or two options to use or have the class work together instead of dividing into small groups.

Step 1

This activity is designed to help students dig deeper into the topic. This section always includes a Bible study.

Step 2

This section offers another way to discover biblical truth.

Step 3

This activity involves the entire class to help students apply what they learned in Steps 1 and 2.

Take It to the Next Level

This final section concludes the session by helping students commit the principles they have learned to their own lives. The question, "So what does this mean to me personally?" can be answered in this section.

Extra Helps

Each unit introduction includes devotion suggestions for the teacher and/or the students. The devotional ideas correlate with the sessions contained in that unit.

Reproducible pages are provided for your convenience. Photocopy these pages for your use or for your students' use to enhance each session.

Additional Resources

The following lists of books and music serve as extra resources for each unit. Feel free to use these materials as research prior to teaching or as extra activities if you deem appropriate.

Unit 1—Peace Talks

How To Talk So Kids Will Listen & Listen So Kids Will Talk by Adele Faber and Elaine Mazlish, Avon Books

Siblings Without Rivalry: How to Help Your Children Live Together So You Can Live Too by Adele Faber and Elaine Mazlish, Avon Books

The New Peoplemaking by Virginia Satir, Science and Behavior Books, Inc.

"Just Between You and Me" by dc Talk (Forefront)

Unit 2—Flak Attack

Parents and Teenagers by Jay Kesler and 50 Christian leaders, Victor Books

Family Communication: Cohesion and Change by Kathleen M. Galvin and Bernard Brommel, Addison-Wesley Educational Books

Reducing School Violence Through Conflict Resolution by David W. Johnson and Roger T. Johnson

Good Behavior by Stephen and Marianne Garber, Robyn Freedman, Villard Books

Unit 3—Ultimate Conflict

The Screwtape Letters by C.S. Lewis, Macmillan Publishing (You may want to use excerpts from this book to read to your class as an introduction to each session.)

Winning Spiritual Warfare by Neil T. Anderson, Harvest House

Steps to Freedom in Christ by Neil T. Anderson, Gospel Light

The Bondage Breaker by Neil T. Anderson, Harvest House (adult or teen version)

The Handbook for Spiritual Warfare by Dr. Ed Murphy, Nelson Publishing

"The Champion" by Carmen (Myrrh)

"A Mighty Fortress" by Glad (Benson). Found also in most hymnbooks.

"The Anchor Holds" by Ray Boltz (Word)

"Just As I Am" by Ray Boltz (Word)

A Ministry of Confident Kids

If the preteens in your group would benefit from more focused help on the issue of decision making, Standard Publishing offers a distinctively Christian support-group curriculum.

Facing My Feelings
Living in My Family
Making Wise Choices
Growing Through Changes

provides help for hurting kids and struggling parents. Written by Linda Kondracki Sibley, the curriculum guide includes support-group session plans for preschool through preteen, plus a parent guide as well. Information for program administrators—complete with reproducible forms—is provided.

FACING MY FEELINGS helps kids and parents understand that:
- All our feelings are OK.
- There are healthy ways to talk about and deal with our feelings.
- We have a feeling vocabulary and ways to label what we are feeling.
- Our feelings tell us when we need to ask for help.
- Jesus understands us, and His presence with us is the greatest source of help we have for facing our feelings.

LIVING IN MY FAMILY helps kids and parents understand that:
- Every family is special and unique.
- There are no perfect families.
- Changes in family life disrupt our sense of security but we can adapt.
- Coping skills help us when our family doesn't or can't meet our needs.
- We need to develop basic skills to communicate in our family.
- Belonging to God's family gives us strength and security.

MAKING WISE CHOICES helps kids and parents understand that:
- We always have choices, no matter what the situation.
- There's a process we can follow to make wise choices.
- God's Spirit with us is our most valuable resource for choosing wisely.
- We can identify wise people who can help us make intelligent choices.

GROWING THROUGH CHANGES helps kids and parents understand that:
- Change is a natural part of God's design for our world.
- There are healthy ways to respond to change.
- Changed circumstances always pass and hurts heal.
- God is a constant friend and guide through every change.

Unit 1
Peace Talks

One of the greatest battlegrounds preteens face is the battleground within their own families. Sibling rivalry and battles with parents can sabotage relationships and make life at home less than God intended it to be. Often at the heart of family battles is an inability to communicate in clear ways, resulting in mixed meanings, misunderstandings, and manipulative behaviors. In this unit, you will have the opportunity to help your preteens conquer this battlefield by teaching them some basic communication skills they can put into practice at home. Sounds simple, doesn't it? But nothing is simple about learning to communicate clearly with others. Nor is one skill more important for your students to learn. Why? Because communication is the single most important way we build, or destroy, relationships.

The material you present in the next few weeks is particularly important to preteens. As they enter the teen years, the battlegrounds at home may escalate—particularly in homes currently lacking good communication. Of course, the entire subject of good family communication is too big a subject to study in-depth within one unit. But during the weeks ahead, you can help your students lay a foundation of basic communication principles and practical strategies that will serve them well as they move through puberty and into the teen years.

Session 1
Know how good communication strengthens family relationships and recognize the common communication barriers (land mines) that "blow up" family relationships.

Feel motivated to strengthen their relationships at home by learning and using better communication skills.

Practice identifying communication land mines and replacing them with peace-making communication.

Session 2
Know a simple formula for sending straight, clear messages.

Feel capable of sending clear messages.

Practice changing unclear, confusing messages into straight, clear messages.

Session 3
Know the four principles of being a good listener.

Feel the desire to be a good listener to others in their families.

Practice using good listening skills.

Session 4
Know biblical principles for responding to family fights.

Feel empowered to minimize fights at home by using good communication skills.

Identify strategies that will help to express anger in appropriate and non-destructive ways.

As you prepare to teach this unit, become familiar with the following information.

1. *Communication* is any means we use to connect with another person. The task of communication is to get what is in my head and heart into your head and heart in such a way that you will understand and feel exactly what I mean to say to you.

2. The *sender* refers to the person who is communicating something to someone else.

3. The *receiver* is the person who is trying to understand what the sender intends to say.

4. A *communication transaction* happens any time a sender sends a message and a receiver receives it. We can think of it as the basic unit of communication. Communication transactions can be words or actions—something I say or do. It may take many communication transactions between a sender and receiver to achieve clear communication.

The key to understanding clear communication lies in the phrase from the first definition above: *in such a way that you will both understand and feel exactly what I mean to say to you.* When we send a message, our natural tendency is to assume that the other person knows exactly what our words and actions mean—after all, since we know what we think and feel when we say or do something, we assume the other person knows too. On the other hand, when we receive a message, we assume we have received it exactly as the sender intended. However, when what was said and how it was heard are different, the communication transaction is incomplete and confusing—which causes relationships to be incomplete and confusing—and the battles begin.

Remember that communication is a skill we learn; no one is born knowing how to communicate well. Because communication is a skill, it takes time and practice to do it well. Throughout the unit you will find opportunities to help your students apply the concepts they are learning to real life situations both in class and in their own families. Maximize the effectiveness of this unit by encouraging them to work hard on the exercises in class and practice their new skills at home during the week.

Session Overviews

Session 1. To begin this unit, your preteens will explore the age-old problem of family battles with siblings and parents. They will identify the basics of good family communication and see how it leads to peaceful and close family relationships.

Session 2. This session will introduce preteens to the basic communication skill of sending straight, clear messages. They will learn a three-part formula for sending clear messages: Say what you mean and mean what you say + make your words and actions match + ask for what you need = a clear message.

Session 3. The second part of good family communication is effective listening—the ability to accurately receive messages sent to us by other family members. This session teaches a four-part formula for good listening: Give your full attention + be sure you understand what the other person is saying + see the situation from the other person's point of view + give a helpful response = good listening.

Session 4. Perhaps the most difficult part of getting along in our families is remembering to use good communication skills during family fights. Since conflicts will always be part of family life, this final session will teach preteens to draw on God's power as they apply biblical principles and good communication skills to family disagreements. Preteens will also learn suggestions for expressing their anger in ways that do not hurt themselves or other family members.

Bridge the Gap. Talking about communicating with our families is one thing; actually doing it is another matter. This session uses communication games and exercises to facilitate family sharing, and sets the groundwork for families to facilitate meaningful family conversations on a regular basis.

Go to Extremes. Since good family communication is a skill that takes lots of time to learn well, this session provides your class with an additional opportunity to review and apply the basic skills learned throughout this unit.

Additional Instructions

Poster Charts. Sessions 1 through **4**, as well as the **Bridge the Gap** session, refer to a poster during the Step 1 segment. All of these charts are supplied for you at the end of this unit introduction on pages 13 and 14. Please refer to them as you prepare for these sessions.

Video Clips. This unit uses many scenarios and role plays to give your students practice in building good communication skills. To add interest for your preteens, video tape clips from some of their favorite programs or movies to illustrate the communication principles. See session plans for more information on choosing an appropriate clip for each week.

Weekly Observation Sheets. Since effective communication is a skill that takes time and practice, each session contains an observation and practice sheet for your students to use at home and return to class the following week. You can greatly increase your students' abilities to internalize the communication principles by "going the extra mile" to motivate them to use these sheets. Emphasize the importance of these at-home activities in the following ways:

1. Participate yourself. Show your students how to use the sheets by filling them out yourself—both in class and at home during the week. Your involvement will show the students that you take the job of learning communication skills seriously.

2. Offer incentives. When handled properly, rewards for filling out and returning their sheets each week can motivate preteens. Choose rewards that will encourage your students, but will *not* discourage students who do not participate. You could have a grab bag of small prizes or treats kids can choose from as they leave each week, or award points that kids can "spend" at the end of the unit for prizes or participation in a special outing.

Skits. This unit includes a number of scripts illustrating both proper and improper communication skills. Your preteens *love* participating in skits, but need time to prepare. Look over the whole unit and become familiar with all the skits so you can invite kids to participate the week before. Give them scripts to take home so they can prepare throughout the week.

Scripture Devotionals

To prepare for this unit, reflect on the following Scriptures as they relate to improving the communication skills in your own life:

Romans 12:18—God's plan is for families to live together peacefully. (Additional verses: Proverbs 12:16, 18; 15:1-18; 16:24; 29:11; Ecclesiastes 5:5; 10:12; Philippians 4:5.)

Matthew 5:37—Be clear in your communication. (Additional verses: Proverbs 12:19; Ecclesiastes 5:5; Ephesians 5:4; James 4:2, 3.)

James 1:19—A good verse to memorize to help us be better listeners. (Additional verses: Proverbs 12:19; Ecclesiastes 5:5; Ephesians 5:4; James 4:2, 3.)

Ephesians 4:26, 27—Instructions for handling anger during times of conflict. (Additional verses: Romans 12:18; Galatians 5:22; Ephesians 4:31, 32; 6:1-3.)

Poster Charts for This Unit

Session 1 Poster

Scripture	Conflict Making	Peace Making
Proverbs 15:1	Harsh words	Gentle words
Proverbs 15:4	Deceitful (lying, tricking)	Words that heal (comfort)
Proverbs 15:18	Hot temper	Patience
Proverbs 12:16	Strikes back when insulted	Ignores insults
Proverbs 12:18	Speaks without thinking	Thinks of helpful words to say
Proverbs 16:24		Speaks pleasantly
Proverbs 29:11	Blows up at others	Does not respond out of anger
Ecclesiastes 5:5	Does not do what they say they will do	Does what they say they will do
Ecclesiastes 10:12	Ungracious (impolite and disrespectful)	Gracious (polite and respectful)
Philippians 4:5		Is gentle to everyone
Romans 12:18		Stays at peace with everyone

Session 2 Poster

Scripture	Don't	Do
Proverbs 12:19	Tell lies, be deceitful	Tell the truth, say words that are true
Ephesians 5:4	Use swear words, say things for shock value (foolish talk) or tell crude jokes	Say "thank you" to others and God
Ecclesiastes 5:5	Say you will do something but never do it	Do the things you say you will do
Matthew 5:37	Say things you don't mean	Say exactly what you mean
James 4:2, 3	Fight, quarrel, and hurt others to get what you want	Ask God for the things you really need

Session 3 Poster

Scripture	Good Listeners	Poor Listeners
Proverbs 18:13		Answer before listening
Proverbs 25:11	Know the right thing to say	
Ecclesiastes 3:7	Know when to be silent	Know when to speak
Ecclesiastes 9:17	Listen and respond quietly	Respond with loud words
Ephesians 4:29	Know how to say what others need to hear	
James 1:19	Are quick to listen	Are quick to speak and get angry

Poster Charts for This Unit

Session 4 Poster

Scripture	Conflict Making	Peace Making
Ephesians 6:1-3		Obey and honor your parents
Ephesians 4:26, 27	Hold on to grudges and express your anger in ways that the devil would want you to	Express anger in non-sinful ways
Ephesians 4:31, 32	Be bitter or full of rage, solve conflicts with fist fights or telling lies about the other person	Be kind, compassionate, and forgiving
Galatians 5:22-26	Be conceited, provoke others to fights, and be envious (especially relates to sibling rivalry)	Live by God's Spirit within you; ask Him to give you the character qualities of the fruit of the Spirit
Romans 12:18		Do your part to live at peace with other family members

Bridge the Gap Poster

Scripture	Good Listeners	Poor Listeners
Proverbs 18:13		Answer before listening
Proverbs 25:11	Know the right thing to say	
Ecclesiastes 3:7	Know when to be silent	Know when to speak
Ecclesiastes 9:17	Listen and respond quietly	Respond with loud words
Ephesians 4:29	Know how to say what others need to hear	
James 1:19	Are quick to listen	Are quick to speak and get angry

Watch Out for Land Mines!

Scripture: Genesis 4:1-11; Proverbs 12:16, 18; 15:1,4,18; 16:24; 29:11; Ecclesiastes 5:5; 10:12; Philippians 4:5
Memory Verse: Romans 12:18

Know how good communication strengthens family relationships and recognize the common communication barriers (land mines) that "blow up" family relationships.
Feel motivated to strengthen their relationships at home by learning and using better communication skills.
Practice identifying communication land mines and replacing them with peace-making communication.

Get Into the Game

Begin this unit on family communication by playing a simple game of charades. In advance write words or short phrases on slips of paper. To play, divide the class into two teams. Have someone from the first team draw a word and act it out within two minutes. Award a point for each word guessed before the timer runs out.

Following the game say, "Today we are learning how to get along better with our families. We'll talk about the ways we communicate with each other: how we talk and listen to each other and how we let others in our families know what we feel and need from them. The game we just played is a communication game. You may have discovered by playing it that communicating with others is not always easy. Your teammates didn't always know what you were trying to tell them by your actions. How did you feel when you were trying to communicate something and your teammates didn't get it?" *(frustrated, impatient, angry)* "Of course the game would have been easier if you could have used words. In real life, even when we use words, we often have the same problems. Family members don't always make themselves clear or understand what others are trying to tell them. They end up feeling frustrated, misunderstood, and even angry. In the weeks ahead, we are going to discover some ways to communicate more clearly within our families."

Step 1

In advance, arrange for players to present the two skits from page 19, and give them scripts to practice. Invite them to pre-

Materials

a list of words or phrases written on slips of paper, a two minute timer

Materials

photocopies of page 19, small table, chairs, two cereal bowls, two spoons, a box of cereal, milk, poster board, marker, Bibles

sent the skits at this time. When they are finished ask, "What differences did you notice in these two families?" *(Let kids respond.)* "Which family would you rather live in?" *(Let kids respond.)* "These two families show the difference between a family that uses good communication skills and one that is stressful and tense because they don't know how to communicate well. Everyone wants to live in a peaceful family. Peace comes from the way we talk to and listen to each other. When we do that well, we have good family communication, and peace fills our families. Communicating well, however, is not automatic; it is a skill we all must learn. We can start by looking at the guidelines for good communication God has given us in the Bible."

Have one or more students read Genesis 4:1-11 aloud. Say, "As you can see, family conflicts have existed since the beginning of time. Every family has them. Sometimes they get so bad the family suffers a great deal. However, when we follow certain rules about how we talk to and listen to each other, we get along better, and our families find peace." Display a poster board with headings as shown on page 13. Ask the class to determine what the verse tells them about conflict-making versus peace-making communication. Write responses on the poster board.

Say, "You can probably see that following God's guidelines for peaceful communication is not easy! Let's see if we can discover more about how these verses relate to living in our families."

Step 2

As an option during the week, record several video clips that illustrate conflict-producing communication styles in families from some of your kids' favorite TV shows or movies. Show them at this time and then say, "Notice how each of the conflicts these families faced is the result of a conflict-making communication style. What did you see?" Ask kids to refer to the poster you made earlier and apply their comments to your video clips. If you cannot use video clips, distribute photocopies of the opening skits and have the kids identify words and phrases that illustrate both conflict-making and peace-making communication as listed on your poster.

Say, "It is hard to get along with others and to have a peaceful family when we use conflict-making communication styles. We can think of them as land mines that have the potential to quickly blow up our relationships and damage our families. Like land mines, we can trigger them without even knowing what we're doing. To avoid these dangerous communication land mines, we need to know what they are. There are many

Materials
video clips of conflict-making communication from kids' favorite TV shows or movies or photocopies of the opening skits on page 19, poster board with the communication land mines listed, slips of paper with several words from Romans 12:18 written on each

of them, and we'll learn more in other weeks. For now, let's start with these." Display a poster listing the following land mines and give an example of each. Feel free to change the following examples to words and actions your preteens actually say and do.

1. Blaming. "It's all your fault! You made me do it!"

2. Harsh language. This includes put downs, name calling, an angry tone of voice. "You creep! If you ever come into my room again I'll smash your face to bits!"

3. Broken promises. This is saying you will do something and not keeping your word, such as telling your mom you'll be home right after school and then going to the park to play ball instead.

4. Responding in anger. This includes hitting, name calling, saying, "I hate you!" and breaking things.

Now say, "Unfortunately, these communication land mines are easier and more natural for us to use than peace-making communication. But God intends for us to live at peace in our families." Distribute slips of paper with several words from the memory verse written on each to class members. Have these kids come to the front of your class and arrange themselves in order. Then have the class read the verse together several times, hiding some of the words each time until kids can say it from memory. Conclude by saying, "Romans 12:18 can help us remember to ask God for help to avoid communication land mines that destroy peace in our families."

Step 3

Before class, photocopy the scenarios on page 20 and cut them apart. Then say, "Avoiding communication land mines and keeping peace in our families is not easy. Changing our communication from conflict making to peace making takes time and practice. Let's try some right now." Invite two volunteers to read the first scenario from page 20. Have class members identify which communication land mine is being used and suggest a replay using peace-making communication. Then have the volunteers replay the scene using the suggested changes. Continue with the next scenarios, inviting new kids to help each time.

Review the poster with the scriptural guidelines on it that you made in Step 1. Say, "God has given us guidelines in the Bible for getting along with our families, but it takes time and practice to learn to use them well. We can have peaceful families when we work hard to eliminate the communication land mines in our families and follow God's guidelines for peace-making communication instead."

Materials
photocopies of page 20, cut apart

Take It to the Next Level

Review today's memory verse, giving special attention to the phrase *as much as it depends on me*. Say, "Having peaceful families requires that all members work together to eliminate communication land mines and replace them with God's guidelines for peacemaking communication. Although you cannot control what other family members will say or do, you can control what you will say and do. God asks us to do whatever we can to live peaceably in our families." Distribute one photocopy of page 21 and ask the kids to write down an instance when they used each communication land mine in their own families. Invite volunteers to share examples from their sheets with the rest of the class.

Use this discussion to lead into a class prayer time. Tell kids that God understands how difficult it can be to change our conflict-making communication into peace-making communication, but He can give us the power to do so. Encourage kids to pray honestly for help with their most difficult communication land mine this week. Use a small notebook as a prayer journal for your class throughout this unit. Keep track of kids' requests today and remember to pray for them during the week.

End your class by distributing a second photocopy of page 21. Instruct kids to use it as an observation sheet to record instances of communication land mines in their families during the week. Encourage them to particularly observe their own communication and note times they replaced a land mine with peace-making communication. Offer a small incentive to anyone who returns a completed sheet next week. (Note: Take a sheet to fill out yourself and share it with the kids next week. This will let your class know that you take the observation sheets seriously, and it will encourage them to practice their communication skills during the week.)

Materials
two photocopies per student of page 21, small notebook, pen or pencil

Two Sets of JONES

Jones Family #1

Mom: *(Standing in front of a table, placing breakfast items out. Yells off stage)* You two better get down here right now! You're going to be late for school again! If I have to call you one more time, you're both grounded!

Jared: *(enters)* Katie's being a brat, as usual! It's her fault I'm late! Tell her to stay out of my room!

Katie: *(enters, hair messy)* I didn't go into your stupid room! Mom, he's such a creep! He locked me out of the bathroom!

Jared: Well, you take forever when you get in there. *(Looks at table.)* Oh yuck! Where's the good cereal? I can't eat this junk. I suppose *she* ate all the Monster Marshmallow Mashers!

Mom: *(looks exasperated)* Jared, don't start with your whining this morning! I'm not in the mood! And Katie, if you don't hurry up we're all going to be late! You haven't even brushed your hair yet!

Katie: *(sarcastically)* I told you, Mom, *he* locked me out of the bathroom! And I did not eat your gross and disgusting Monster Marshmallow Mashers!

Mom: OK, that's it! Go get your things for school. We're leaving right now! I can't take anymore of this from either of you!

(all exit, kids mumbling "now see what you've done," "but I'm hungry," etc.)

Jones Family #2

Mom: *(Standing in front of a table, placing breakfast items out. Yells off stage).* Time for breakfast, you two! It's getting late!

Brian: *(enters)* Mom, Sara's being slow again. She took about an hour in the bathroom!

Mom: Let me worry about Sara, Brian. You need to eat your cereal.

Sara: *(enters)* OK, world! I'm ready for you!

Brian: *(rolls his eyes, says teasingly)* Yeah, but is the world ready for you? Hey, Mom, where are the Choc-O-Flakes?

Mom: I'm sorry, honey, but I couldn't get to the store yesterday. You'll have to settle for these today.

Brian: Oh, all right. Can we get some more today?

Sara: Mom, I forgot! I have a permission slip you need to sign for the field trip next week. I have to bring it back with two dollars today!

Mom: Sara! Why do you always wait until the last minute to tell me these things? Bring it in the car, and I'll take care of it there. *(Looks her right in the eyes)* Now listen to me, young lady. I need you to take responsibility to give me things like this as soon as they come home from school. The next time you spring this on me, you'll have to take it in late. OK?

Brian: Yeah, Noodle Brain! You're gonna get what you deserve, at last!

Mom: Don't start, Brian. This is not about you. Now, both of you have two minutes to get your stuff and meet me in the garage. Let's go, gang! *(All exit)*

Diffusing Land Mines

Scenario #1

Mom: Joey, you spilled your milk again! Go get the dish cloth and clean it up!

Joey: It's not my fault, Mom! If you hadn't filled the glass so full I wouldn't have spilled it! Why should I have to clean it up when it wasn't my fault?

Communication land mine:
Blaming

Suggested Replay:

Joey: I'm sorry, Mom. I'll clean it up.

Scenario #2

Dad: Maria, didn't you promise me you were going to do your chores right after supper? That was three hours ago, and they're still not done.

Maria: I guess I forgot.

Dad: Well turn off the TV right now and go do them!

Maria: No! This is my favorite show! I'll do them before I go to bed. I promise!

Communication land mine:
Broken promises, not doing what you say you will do.

Suggested Replay:

Maria: I'm sorry, Dad. I'll do them right now.

Scenario #3

Younger brother: Mom! Jason ripped my school picture out of my hands! Tell him to give it back!

Older brother: What a cry baby! Nobody cares about your stupid picture! I'm going to rip it up and flush it down the toilet! Try and stop me, cry baby!

Communication land mine:
Harsh, unkind language

Suggested Replay:

Older brother: OK! OK! I just wanted to see it. Here's your picture; you can have it back!

Scenario #4

Younger sister: Daddy! Jessica hit me really hard!

Older sister: She deserved it, Dad! She messed up our *Scrabble* board just because she was losing! You're a cheater, Lisa, and I don't ever want to play with you again!

Younger sister: It was an accident! I slipped! I didn't mean to do it!

Communication land mine:
Responding in anger

Suggested Replay:

Older sister: Lisa! You messed up the board!

Lisa: I'm sorry! I slipped! I'll set it up again and give you extra points.

Older sister: No! I know you didn't mean to, but I'm really mad anyway. I don't want to play right now.
(walks away)

Watch out for Land Mines

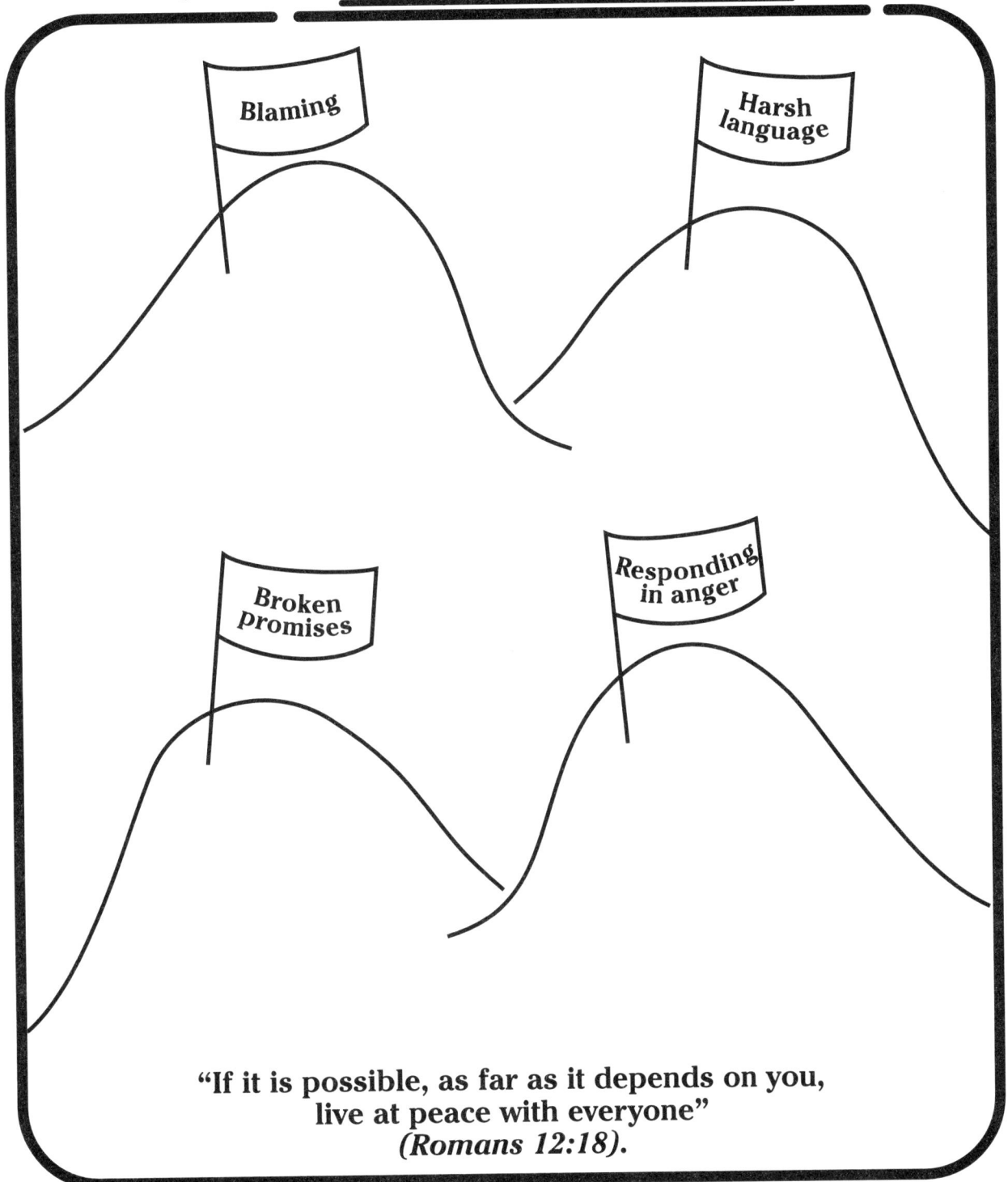

Blaming

Harsh language

Broken promises

Responding in anger

"If it is possible, as far as it depends on you, live at peace with everyone" *(Romans 12:18).*

Make Yourself Perfectly Clear

Scripture: Genesis 27; Proverbs 12:19; Ecclesiastes 5:5; Ephesians 5:4; James 4:2

Memory Verse: Matthew 5:37

Know a simple formula for sending straight, clear messages.

Feel capable of sending clear messages.

Practice changing unclear, confusing messages into straight, clear messages.

Get Into the Game

Give each class member a sheet of paper and have them number from one to seventeen. Read the following list and have kids write down an example for each of the following words. Do *not* tell them how you will use the words and have them keep their choices secret: 1. holiday, 2. month, 3. noun, 4. animal, 5. famous person, 6. color, 7. a country, 8. a sport, 9. famous sports star, 10. noun, 11. a kind of store (department, hardware, grocery, etc.), 12. adjective, 13. noun, 14. adjective, 15. noun, 16. number, 17. verb ending in "ing" (cleaning, eating, walking, etc.)

Then have kids number off from one to seventeen. As you read the following story, have Student 1 fill in the blank with the first word on his list; Student 2 will fill in the second blank, and so on throughout the story. If time allows, assign kids a different number and repeat. Notice how the story changes as different words are used in each blank. Then read through the story one more time, asking kids to choose words that actually fit in the blanks so the story makes sense.

The Vacation

The Smith family had a great (1) _____ vacation, which they took last (2) _____. They all piled into their (3) _____, including Fido, their pet (4) _____ and started the long drive to their first stop, Washington D.C. There they visited President (5)_____ who lives in the (6) _____ House. Then they drove to (7)_____ where they had a great time playing (8) _____ with (9) _____ in a (10) _____. Before they started home, they picked up some souvenirs at the (11) _____ store. They bought a (12)

Materials

paper, pens or pencils

_____ (13) _____ and a (14) _____ (15)
_____ . When they got home after (16) _____ days on
the road, they all decided the best part of the trip was (17)
_____ back home again.

Conclude your opening time by saying, "We laughed when
we filled in the blanks of our story with words that didn't fit the
meaning of the sentence. We didn't mind being confused or
frustrated for a while because we knew we were only playing
a game. When it comes to communicating in our families,
however, feeling confused or frustrated because we don't
understand what someone's words or actions mean is *not* fun.
It is another communication land mine that can lead to lots of
hurt feelings and serious misunderstandings. Today we will talk
about how to avoid unclear and confusing communication in
our families by learning to send straight, clear messages to
each other."

Step 1

Say, "One of the most important parts of having good communication in our families is learning how to give clear messages
to each other. What does it mean to 'send a message' to others
in our families?" *(Let kids respond.)* "When we're talking about
communication, a message is anything we try to get across to
another person. We can use words or actions to help others
understand what we are thinking, feeling, or needing from
them. Let's think of some examples. Remember, both words
and actions are communication messages."

Go around the room and ask each student to give specific
examples of a communication message. Examples would be
telling someone about a fight that happened at school, telling
how you feel about getting a *D* on a test, getting your parents to
understand how much you want a certain Christmas gift, getting your little sister to leave you alone, hitting your little sister
for not leaving you alone (a non-verbal message), pouting
when you don't get your way.

"The tricky part of sending communication messages is getting the other person to understand what we are trying to tell
him or her. The key is in how we send the message. When we
send clear messages, other family members never have to
wonder what we are trying to say to them or feel confused by
the way we act towards them. However, when we send messages that are *not* clear, other family members are confused
and don't respond as we would like them to. For instance, in
the examples, firmly telling your little sister that you want her
to leave you alone is a clear message. Hitting her is a confusing
message; she doesn't know what you mean by your action or

Materials
video camera, VCR, and TV (optional),
poster board with headings and references printed out in advance, Bibles

what you want her to do. Telling your parents how you feel about getting a *D* on a test is a clear message. Pouting at the supper table is a confusing message. We'll see more examples of unclear messages in a few minutes. First, let's see what God's Word tells us about using direct messages."

Divide your class into two groups. Give each group one of the following assignments and allow time for them to prepare to share it during Step 2. Circulate between the two groups to be sure they understand their assignment and to offer assistance when needed. (Note: If your class is small, work together on the first project and keep the poster for later.)

Group #1: Prepare a presentation of Genesis 27. This is the story of Jacob and Esau, an example of deceitful, unclear family communication and its result on the family. Have kids read the passage and prepare to present it to the rest of the class. The easiest way to do this is for one or two kids to act as narrators and read the passage while the others pantomime the action. Other options would be to prepare it as a news broadcast or to illustrate it with a series of drawings. (Optional: If you have a video camera, tell kids you will record the final production. This will add interest and help them take the assignment more seriously.)

Group #2: Prepare a poster of God's Do's and Don'ts for clear communication. In advance, print the headings and references on a poster board. Then have the kids look up each verse and fill in the rest of the poster. The completed poster should resemble the one on page 13.

Step 2

When both groups have finished their assignments, have kids make their presentation of Jacob and Esau. Then say, "Families have suffered the effects of poor communication since the beginning of time. Jacob and Rebekah used deceitful communication to get what they wanted from Isaac. What was the result on the total family?" *(Isaac and Esau were deeply hurt; Esau was so angry he vowed to kill his brother; Jacob had to run away from home.)* "This family suffered a great deal from the poor communication of two members. They could have avoided that if they would have followed God's Do's and Don'ts for clear communication."

Have Group 2 make its presentation at this time. If your whole class worked on the skit, display the poster and have kids look up the verses and fill in the blanks together. Say, "We can take God's Do's and Don'ts and write them into three important rules for sending clear messages."

1. Say what you mean and mean what you say. Use words

Materials
poster board, marker, poster of the formula for sending clear messages, last session's poster of the communication land mines

that clearly state what you want to say. No one should have to guess what your words mean.

2. Make your words and actions match. Do what you say you will do. No one will ever trust you if you say one thing and do something different. If you tell your mom you'll be home right after school, don't come in an hour late!

3. Ask for what you need. Be clear about what you want and need others to do. Don't use pouting, fighting, or pretending to be sick to get what you need.

"These three rules make up a formula for sending clear messages. It looks like this: Say what you mean + make your words and actions match + ask for what you need = a clear message. When you are careful to use the formula for clear messages, others in your family will know exactly what you are trying to say to them. If you don't, you will have misunderstandings and conflict in your family." Display the poster of communication land mines you started last week and briefly review them. Then add "unclear, confusing messages" to the list. Conclude by referring to Matthew 5:37, today's memory verse. Say, "This verse is a simple reminder of God's instruction to use understandable messages." Say it together several times.

Step 3

Say, "Let's look at some examples of unclear messages and practice changing them into direct messages."

Distribute photocopies of the cartoons on page 27. Have kids work in pairs to change each confusing message into a clear message. Some examples of clear messages are listed below.

Cartoon: Why can't we ever have anything good for dinner?

Clear message: I'm tired of casseroles for dinner. Can we have turkey tomorrow night?

Cartoon: Math is the dumbest subject in the whole world! Who needs it, anyway?

Clear message: Mom, will you please help me with this math problem? I can't figure it out.

Cartoon: I hate you! I'm never going to talk to you again in my whole life!

Clear message: I'm really disappointed that you didn't come to my school program. You promised you'd come and you didn't.

Materials
video clips (optional), photocopies of page 27, pens or pencils

Take It to the Next Level

Ask kids to report on their observation sheets from this past week; begin by sharing yours with the class. If you offered a small incentive for returning it, award incentives as kids leave. Encourage those who did not fill out the form to do so this week, reminding them that good communication in our families is a skill that takes time and practice to learn well.

Distribute one photocopy of page 28 and have students look at the cartoons. Look at the first frame and write a confusing message in the bubble. Now look at the second frame and write a clearer message and response.

Now ask kids to write one example of a time they used confusing communication with a parent or sibling. Share an example from your own life. Then distribute a second photocopy for kids to take home. Ask them to record a time this week when they sent an unclear message to a family member, and how they changed it (or could have changed it) into a clear one.

Conclude with a prayer time. Use your prayer journal to check up on last week's requests and to ask kids to suggest new requests. Close in prayer and ask God to help each student improve his communication skills at home.

Materials

your copy of the last session's observation sheet, photocopies of page 28, prayer journal, pen or pencil

WHAT Did You Say?

Make Yourself Perfectly Clear

Say what you mean + make your words and actions match + ask for what you need = a clear message

What happened

What I said

How I changed (or could have changed) it to a clear message

"Simply let your 'Yes' be 'Yes,' and your 'No,' 'No'; anything beyond this comes from the evil one" *(Matthew 5:37).*

Session 3

Listen Up!

Scripture: Proverbs 18:13; 25:11;
 Ecclesiastes 3:7; 9:17; Ephesians 4:29
Memory Verse: James 1:19

Know the four principles of being a good
 listener.
Feel the desire to be a good listener to
 others in their families.
Practice using good listening skills.

Get Into the Game

Have everyone sit in a circle. Begin by whispering a phrase into one of the kids' ears. That person must then whisper the same phrase into the ear of the next person. But he can only whisper it once; no repeats! If the student receiving the message did not hear it correctly, he must whisper whatever he thinks he heard. When the phrase reaches the last person, she repeats it aloud. The message has probably changed as it has gone around the circle. Repeat the process as long as time remains. Use phrases from nursery rhymes, songs, or movies. ("All I want for Christmas is my two front teeth" or "Let's pick up seashells at the seashore").

After you have played this game say, "How many of you did not understand what the person next to you whispered into your ear?" *(Let kids respond.)* "What happened when you passed along what you *thought* you heard?" *(The true meaning was lost, and everyone following you was prevented from hearing the real phrase.)*

"Today we will talk about the importance of family members listening to each other. Last week we talked about how to send clear messages. Today we want to look at the other side of good communication—being the one to receive messages. What we hear others say to us and what they actually meant to say can often be very different. By learning to listen carefully, we can avoid many misunderstandings and hurt feelings in our families."

Step 1

Say, "Have you ever told someone in your family, 'You're not listening to me!' What do you mean when you say that to another person?" *(It can mean they are doing something else and not giving full attention, or that the other person did not understand what we meant to say; they may have heard the words, but they didn't understand the meaning).* Invite students to present the first skit from page 34. Then ask each class member to vote "Yes" or "No" to this question: "Was the father listening to the daughter?" Keep track of the responses. Then ask kids to explain why they voted as they did.

"True listening is not just hearing words; it's understanding exactly what the other person meant to say. The father in the first skit thought he was listening. But he was so busy talking, he never let his daughter tell him what she wanted to say. Let's ask our players to redo this scene and make the father a better listener."

Have players present the second skit. Then ask each class member to vote again on whether or not the father was listening to his daughter. Ask kids to identify what he did differently to be a better listener *(let his daughter talk; could hear the details of what happened and how his daughter felt about the fight at school).*

"This is an example of the careful listening that can help us get along better with our families. This kind of listening is a skill we have to learn. We can learn about it by looking at what the Bible says."

Have kids practice listening as they do the following Scripture search. Display the chart with only the Scripture reference and headings filled in. Then divide kids into pairs and instruct one student in each pair to read the first verse to his partner. The listener must then say what the verse teaches about listening skills and note it on a sheet of paper. Then have the pairs switch roles and do the next verse, and so on until they have read all the verses. When all are finished, ask them to report on their conclusions. As they share, record their findings on the poster (see page 13).

The last verse, James 1:19, is a good summary verse to help kids remember to be good listeners. Teach it at this time, using a memory verse game the kids enjoy or the following game:

Write the verse on a chalkboard. Have one class member read the first word of the verse aloud. Then have the next person read the second word, and so on. Read the verse several times in this manner until the kids can say it quickly and smoothly. Then erase half of the words, and repeat, having kids fill in the missing words. When they

Materials

photocopies of page 34, Bible search chart with only the references and headings written out, Bibles, chalkboard, chalk, paper, pens or pencils can do this smoothly, erase the remaining words and repeat until they can say it smoothly.

Step 2

Say, "As you can see from our Bible study, listening involves two things: *hearing* what the other person said and *responding* appropriately. Unfortunately, we often get this backwards; we want to *respond* to the other person *before* we *hear* what they are trying to tell us. But we can't respond appropriately unless we hear what the other person is trying to say. We can follow these rules to help us be better listeners."

1. Give your full attention. Look at others when they are talking to you; don't do anything else. For instance, if your mom is trying to tell you something while you're watching TV, stop looking at the TV screen and look directly at her.

2. Ask questions. When we are listening, we don't usually understand everything right away. We need to ask questions to be sure we understand properly. For instance, if your little brother spills a glass of water on your homework, you can ask, "Did you do that on purpose?" Maybe it really was an accident! Or if your mom tells you to clean up your room but she didn't say when, ask, "When am I supposed to do it? Can it wait until Saturday?"

3. Try to understand what the other person feels. When we listen to others, our first response is to react to our feelings without thinking about what the other person is feeling. Good listeners, however, ask themselves, "If that were me, how would I feel?"

For instance, suppose your mom yelled at you about cleaning your room because she has already asked you to do it three times, and you've ignored her. Ask yourself, "How do I feel when I ask Mom to do something for me three times, and she just ignores me?" *(Let kids answer this question: frustrated, angry.)* "What would I like her to do for me?" *(Do, or at least respond to, what I asked her to do.)*

4. Respond helpfully. If we followed the first three rules, we will be ready to give a helpful response. Responses can be words or actions, depending on the situation. Help kids brainstorm examples of both helpful and unhelpful responses for some of the examples used above.

Your little brother spills a glass of water on your homework. Unhelpful—scream at him, hit him, call him names. Helpful—ask, "Did you do that on purpose?" or "Go get a towel and help me clean this." Or "I know it was an accident, but I'm mad because I have to do it all over. Please leave me alone and let me finish my homework."

Materials
posters of communication land mines and formula for sending clear messages from last session, poster of formula for good listening

Your mom yelled at you about cleaning up your room. Unhelpful—continue to ignore her, yell back, give excuses, pout. Helpful—say "I'm sorry" and get it done!

Guide your students to think of other responses. Unhelpful responses—screaming, hitting, teasing, ignoring, "I forgot," "It's no big deal!" "Get off my case!" Helpful responses—"I'm sorry" "How can I help you?" "You did a great job!" give a hug, do something nice for the other person.

Review the poster of the formula for sending clear messages from the last session. Add a poster with the following formula and say, "Here is a formula for being good listeners: Give full attention + ask questions + understand other's feelings + give a helpful response = good listening." Then refer to the poster of communication land mines from last session and add, "Not listening." Summarize by reminding kids of today's memory verse. Being quick to listen and slow to speak or get angry will make us good listeners and help bring peace to our families!

Step 3

As an option, record several video clips that illustrate good listening skills and poor listening skills from some of your kids' favorite TV shows or movies. Talk about what made the characters good or poor listeners. If you do not have video clips, use the following activity.

Say, "Let's practice using good listening skills." Divide kids into pairs and give each pair a slip of paper with one of the following role plays written on it. Allow time for each pair to create a short skit of the scene using poor communication skills. Ask one pair to present its skit to the rest of the class. Then let the class brainstorm ideas as to how the characters could use the formula for good listening to improve the interaction. Repeat with the other pairs. Then let kids work in pairs again to rewrite their role plays using the formula for good listening. Invite several pairs to share their new skits with the class.

1. You and your mom are disagreeing in a store about an outfit you want to buy.

2. Your little brother and his friend want to play street hockey with you and your friend.

3. Your dad is yelling at you because you came home from school an hour late.

Materials
video clips (optional), role play starters written out on slips of paper

Take It to the Next Level

Ask kids to report on their observation sheets from this past week; begin by sharing yours with the class. If you offered small incentives, award those as kids leave. Encourage those

Materials
your photocopy of last week's observation sheet, photocopies of page 35, prayer journal

who did not fill out a sheet to do so this week, reminding them that good communication in our families is a skill that takes time and practice to learn.

Distribute two photocopies of page 35 to each student. Ask kids to write one example of a time they did not listen when a parent or sibling was talking to them. Share an example from your own life. Ask students to take the second sheet home and to record a time this week when they listen well to another family member.

Conclude with a prayer time. Use your prayer journal to check on last week's requests. Ask kids to suggest new requests. Close in prayer, asking God to help each class member improve communication skills at home.

Are You Listening?

Skit #1

Kim: Hey Daddy, want to hear what happened at school today?

Dad: (reading a newspaper) Umm. Sure, honey.

Kim: Well, there was this big fight on the playground during recess...

Dad: (puts paper down) A fight? Where? When?

Kim: I just told you, on the playground during recess. But you know what happened? This boy started...

Dad: Wasn't there a teacher around?

Kim: No, not just then. But wait, let me tell you...

Dad: Where was the teacher?

Kim: (frustrated) I don't know where the teacher was! Would you just listen!

Dad: (sternly) You know how I feel about fights, Kim. I better not hear that you were involved!

Kim: (walks away) Oh, forget it! You never listen to me.

Dad: (surprised) What do you mean? I'm listening!

Skit #2

Kim: Hey Daddy, want to hear what happened at school today?

Dad: (puts newspaper down) Sure, honey. What's up?

Kim: Well, there was this big fight on the playground during recess...

Dad: Really?

Kim: Yeah! This boy started to hit another boy and missed and hit this other kid instead. So the other kid hit him back, but he missed too and hit another kid! Pretty soon there were six kids all fighting together!

Dad: Sounds like quite a scene. Wasn't there a teacher around?

Kim: She came later. The whole school came later!

Dad: Umm.

Kim: I was scared for a minute that someone might punch me!

Dad: Fighting can easily get out of hand. But you can always walk away!

Kim: Yeah. It was pretty exciting, though!

Dad: I guess so! Thanks for telling me about it, Kim!

Listen Up!

"My dear brothers, take note of this: Everyone should be quick to listen, slow to speak and slow to become angry" (James 1:19).

What happened:

_____

_____

_____

_____

_____

What I said:

_____

_____

_____

_____

What I did (or could have done) to be a better listener:

_____

_____

_____

_____

_____

_____

_____

Give full attention + ask questions +
understand other's feelings +
give a helpful response = good listening

Cease Fire!

Scripture: Romans 12:18; Galatians 5:22;
Ephesians 4:31, 32; 6:1-3
Memory Verse: Ephesians 4:26, 27

Know biblical principles for responding
to family fights.
Feel empowered to minimize fights at
home by using good communication
skills.
Identify strategies that will help to
express anger in appropriate and
non-destructive ways.

Get Into the Game

Activity #1

As your students arrive, direct them to a wall where you
have attached a strip of butcher or shelf paper with "Family
Fights" written in big letters across the center. Ask kids to add
words or pictures depicting their thoughts and feelings about
the title. Here are some suggestions to get kids started: phrases
said in your homes during fights, pictures of a family disagreement, words that depict your feelings during family fights.

Activity #2

Set up a table with another strip of paper and lots of news
magazines and newspapers. Instruct kids to make a mural by
attaching to the paper any articles or pictures that depict the
results of fighting—including global wars, community violence,
and domestic conflicts. When the paper is full of articles, take
a wide tip marker and write "Stop the Violence" in bold letters
across the front. Display the mural next to the graffiti board.

Summarize the opening activities by saying, "Perhaps the
hardest part of bringing peace to our families is what we do
and say when we disagree. No one likes to fight and get upset
with other family members; look at what we wrote on our graffiti board about it." Refer to specific words and phrases on the
graffiti board. "Unfortunately, however, as long as families are
made of human beings, they will have disagreements and
fights. It is part of our human nature to respond to differences
and disagreements by fighting. Look at all the articles we found
for our mural! The problem is not having differences and disagreements. How people respond to them determines whether
peace or destruction is in our world. Our mural shows the

Materials

two 3' strips of butcher or shelf paper,
news magazines and newspapers,
markers

result of using violence and anger to solve disagreements, but it doesn't have to be that way! Of course, we can't bring peace to all the world's conflicts today, but we can start by using all we've learned about good family communication to peacefully resolve disagreements in our homes."

Step 1

Divide students into pairs. Give them two minutes to write instances they have seen in TV programs, movies, or video games of conflicts being solved with violence. Have kids share their lists with each other. Then say, "People seem to like violence in TV shows or movies or video games. What do you like about _____?" Choose shows and games your kids listed most often. Answers will probably be about the special effects or the satisfaction when the good guys blow away the bad guys.

Say, "Special effects are fun to watch in the fantasy world of media. However, when we settle disputes in our homes with anger and violence, our families are blown away. It doesn't have to be that way. God has given us many guidelines for handling differences in ways that bring peace, instead of hurt, to our families."

Display a poster board with the headings from the **Session 4** Poster from page 14 written on it. Then have kids read the listed verses one at a time. If your kids are good at finding verses, they could look for them in a sword drill fashion. Call out the reference and let the first one to find it read it aloud. Then ask the class to determine what the verse tells them about handling conflict in their homes. Write responses on your poster, including the following information.

Say, "These verses give us powerful teaching on how to live in our families. However, putting it into practice is hard. When we are fighting with a brother or sister, the last thing we want to do is be kind and compassionate and forgiving. We'd rather respond in rage. But what does Galatians 5:24 tell us?" *(Let kids respond. If we belong to Christ, He puts to death our old, sinful nature.)* "In other words, we have God's power to respond according to His rules rather than Satan's rules!

"Our key verses for today are Ephesians 4:26, 27. They summarize what God teaches us about handling conflict in our families. The key phrase is 'in your anger, do not sin.' God knows that we will always have disagreements and get angry, but He also knows that we can choose how we handle our disagreements. We can hold on to grudges and respond hurtfully, or we can ask God to give us His power to respond in ways that lead to peace in our families."

Materials
poster board, or Bibles, paper, pens or pencils

Step 2

As an option, record several video clips from some of your kids' favorite TV shows or movies that illustrate family fights. If you do not have video clips, let several kids prepare "The Day After Christmas" skit from page 42. Then ask the following questions. "Does any of this sound familiar?" *(Let kids respond)* "What is the problem here?" *(Older brother does not want to give in to his younger brother.)* "Look at our poster of biblical principles. Which ones did Rick violate?" *(All of them)* "What was the result?" *(All three family members are upset, and Rick has to spend time in his room.)*

Refer to the posters of communication land mines and good communication formulas from previous weeks as you present the following. Say, "It's hard enough to remember to use good communication skills in normal situations. It's even harder to remember to use them when we are upset. During those times, our first reaction is to use all these communication land mines. The key to having peace in our families lies in using good communication skills even when we are angry. Instead of responding with the land mines, we need to follow several steps."

1. Give clear messages. Refer to the formula for sending clear messages. When we are having a fight, we tend to say things that are not clear or helpful. Saying, "I can if I want to!" or "Oh, yeah? Just try and make me!" doesn't mean anything. Rather, we need to express what we feel or what we want from the other person.

2. Listen to the other person's point of view. Refer to the formula for being good listeners. When we fight, we tend to react without thinking or knowing the whole story. Remember that good listening involves asking questions and seeing things from the other person's perspective. This is especially important when we are upset. You can ask yourself, "How does my brother (or sister or mom or dad) feel right now? What does he need from me?"

3. Work it out peaceably. Many fights end with hurt feelings and sometimes hurt bodies! But you can end a fight with a peaceful settlement, even if you have to wait until everyone's feelings have calmed down. Sometimes the hardest words to say are "I'm sorry" or "Let's do it your way this time." Just remember that working things out peaceably is your choice.

4. Draw on God's power. None of this is easy. If it was, our world wouldn't display so much violence. As Christians, however, we have a secret weapon! God's Spirit within us can provide the power for us to handle our fights. Ask God to grow the fruit of the Spirit in you and see the difference it makes in living with your family!

Materials
video clips (optional), photocopies of page 42, toy truck and a *Game Boy*, posters of communication land mines and formulas, new poster of the formula for a peaceful family

Display the poster of the following formula and say, "Putting all this into another formula looks like this: Give clear messages + listen to the other person's point of view + work things out = a peaceful family."

(Note: Adapt this next section to fit any video clips you used.) Put kids into groups of three and give them photocopies of the first part of "The Day After Christmas." Instruct each group to plan another version of the skit, showing how Rick could have handled this situation peaceably. Have them present their completed skits to the rest of the class. Here are some suggestions:

1. Give clear messages. "I think your truck is neat. Can I use it for a few minutes?"

2. Listen to the other person's point of view. "I would want my stuff back if I asked for it; he has a right to his stuff."

3. Work it out. "Do you want to play with my road racer while I play with your truck?" or simply give it back without a hassle.

4. Draw on God's power to do it. Rick can ask God to give him the fruit of the Spirit so he can respond peacefully to his brother in the future.

Conclude by having your players present the second part of "The Day After Christmas," which includes the above suggestions. Compare this version with the ones your kids wrote and note the differences. Point out that Rick could have followed several options to resolve this disagreement.

Step 3

Say, "The hardest part about communicating well during family fights is that when we are angry, we instinctively react without thinking and lash out with harsh words or punches. However, we don't have to let that happen; we can learn to make better choices when we feel ourselves getting angry. Always remember that what you do when you feel angry is a choice you make; no one makes you use harsh words or throw a punch!" Review Ephesians 4:26, 27, asking kids to list responses to anger that would be sinful (i.e., screaming at others, calling them names, hitting, breaking things, telling lies, refusing to do what parents ask). Then place a box containing a pillow, punching bag, running shoes, paper, pens and pencils, markers, and a sign saying, "I'm sorry," in the center of your table. Say, "We can never remember to give clear messages and listen to the other person's point of view when we let our anger speak for us. Rather, we can always control our anger by finding a safe way to express it." Bring out the items from your box individually, asking kids to think of a way they can use each one to express their anger. Here are some suggestions:

Materials
box, a pillow, a punching bag, running shoes, paper, pens or pencils, markers, a sign saying, "I'm sorry"

1. Pillow—scream into it or punch it.

2. Punching bag—punch it.

3. Running shoes—run around the block once or twice.

4. Paper, pens and pencils, markers—write a letter to the person (*but don't send it*), journal, or draw a picture of your anger.

5. "I'm sorry"—if you have done something harmful in your anger, apologize; never just ignore it.

Say, "When you feel your anger rising, you can walk away from the situation and find a safe way to express it. When you and the other family members have calmed down, get together again and resolve the issues. This is not easy, but you can do it—especially when you ask God to help."

Ask volunteers to read the following sentences aloud and then choose one item from the table that the character could use to express her anger safely.

1. Joseph is really mad because his older sister ripped up his homework just to be mean. He wants to rip hers too.

2. Rachel's mom yelled at her for not doing the dishes. She knows it's her brother's night to do them, but her mom wouldn't listen. Rachel wants to throw the dishes against the wall instead of putting them in the dishwasher.

3. Annette's little sister wants to watch a Sesame Street video. Annette is interested in the show she's watching, but her dad makes her start the video. She wants to punch her sister and yell at her dad.

4. Tom received a phone message that his dad wouldn't be able to see him this weekend. This is the third time in a row his dad has done this, and Tom is so angry he wants to throw everything near the phone—the answering machine, the lamp, and anything else nearby!

Conclude by saying, "Remember, making choices about what to do when you are angry is not easy! But you can do it, with God's help." Use a memory verse activity to help your kids memorize Ephesians 4:26, 27.

Take It to the Next Level

Ask kids to report on using their "Listen Up!" observation sheets at home this past week. Share yours with the class. If you offered an incentive, award those as kids leave.

Distribute photocopies of page 43 to the kids. First, have them name one or two specific fights they have had at home and what they did to express their anger. For instance, did they yell at a parent, hit a sibling, break something, pout, or hold a grudge? Next, have them circle several options on how to express their anger safely. Be sure they choose options that they would actually do. Share an example of how you handle

Materials
your copy of last week's observation sheet, photocopies of page 43, prayer journal

anger. Then have them write a prayer, asking for God's power to help them use good communication skills with their families. Encourage your students that even though this session ends your unit, they can keep trying to send clear messages, be good listeners, and settle disagreements peaceably at home.

Conclude with a prayer time. Use your prayer journal to check on this unit's past prayer requests. Close in prayer, asking God to help each class member continue to improve his communication at home.

The Day After Christmas

Characters:
Rick, his younger brother, Aaron, and his mom
(Scene: Rick is playing with Aaron's truck; Aaron is standing beside him, very upset.)

Part 1

Aaron: Rick! Give me my truck back! It was my Christmas present, not yours! You promised to give it back a long time ago! You've had it for an hour!

Rick: Oh yeah, right! I'll give it back when I'm good and ready! Get out of here, you little brat! *(pushes Aaron so hard he falls over backwards)*

Aaron: Mom! *(yells as he runs from the room)*

Mom: *(enters, with Aaron)* Rick, give Aaron his truck back. Didn't you get enough stuff of your own?

Rick: *(continues playing with the truck without looking at his mom)* I'm not hurting it! He's got other stuff too! Tell the little creep to go play with something else!

Mom: *(Picks up a Game Boy and gives it to Aaron)* OK, then Aaron can play with this for as long as he wants.

Rick: Mom, what are you doing? That's my *Game Boy*! He doesn't even know how to use it! He'll break it! *(grabs Game Boy and shoves Aaron again)*

Mom: OK, that's it. Leave all your things here and go to your room. Don't come out until I tell you to!

Rick: *(throws truck down and stomps off, yelling)* You're mean and it's not fair! It's all his fault; he should have left me alone and everything would be fine! Why aren't you punishing him?

Part 2

Aaron: Rick! Give me my truck back! It was my Christmas present, not yours! You promised to give it back a long time ago!

Rick: I think your truck is cool. Can I just use it for a few more minutes?

Aaron: You've had it for an hour already! Mom! *(yells as he runs from the room)*

Mom: *(enters, with Aaron)* Rick, give Aaron his truck back. Didn't you get enough stuff of your own?

Rick: But I like it! I just want to use it for awhile. Hey, Aaron, do you want to play with my road racer while I play with your truck?

Aaron: No! I want my truck.

Mom: Rick...

Rick: OK, OK. Here's your truck, Aaron. I guess I'd want my stuff back if I asked for it.

Mom: Thank you, Rick. Hey, guys! I still have some Christmas cookies left from yesterday. Anyone want a snack?

Boys: Sure! *(exit)*

Cease Fire!

"In your anger do not sin: Do not let the sun go down while you are still angry, and do not give the devil a foothold"
(Ephesians 4:26, 27).

Circle the picture(s) of things you can do instead of being angry.

When I am angry, I usually

_____
_____
_____
_____
_____

Dear God,

_____
_____
_____
_____
_____

Give clear messages + listen to the other person's point of view + work things out = a peaceful family

Bridge the Gap

Can We Talk?

Scripture: Proverbs 18:13; 25:11;
Ecclesiastes 3:7; 9:17; Ephesians 4:29;
James 1:19

Know the importance of good family
communication and basic principles
for family sharing times.
Feel motivated to spend time in meaningful family conversations.
Identify subjects kids and parents would
like to talk about in future family sharing times.

Get Into the Game

Activity #1

As participants arrive, direct them to make their own name
tags. Provide items for decoration, such as stickers, rubber
stamps, ribbon, and glitter. Encourage everyone to decorate
their tags in ways that have meaning to them (i.e. a sticker or
stamp of a favorite food or animal, a ribbon border in a favorite
color).

Activity #2

When all participants have made a name tag, give everyone
paper and pencil and ask them to scatter around the room so
that family members are not sitting next to each other. Read
the following list of questions, asking participants to write their
answers on one side of the paper:
  1. What is your favorite color?
  2. What is the name of your workplace or school?
  3. What do you do when you are really sleepy? For instance,
do you slip away and quietly go to bed, get crabby, or fall
asleep on the couch?
  4. Name one thing that makes you angry.
  5. What is your favorite food?
  6. Who is your greatest hero (heroine)?
  7. What is your favorite thing to do with the rest of your family?

Materials
name tags, stickers, rubber stamps,
ribbon, glitter, glue or paste

8. Name one thing that makes you happy.

9. If you could be any animal you wanted to be, which would you choose?

10. What was your favorite Christmas gift last year?

Now read through the list again, instructing participants to write next to their answers how *they think their parent or preteen answered the questions.* When all have answered, ask participants to rejoin their family members. Now read through the list again, asking participants to compare their lists and give themselves a point for each time their answers matched. Allow enough time between each question for family members to talk about their answers. Then have families tally their points and applaud the family who scored the highest.

Say, "During this unit, we have talked about communicating in our families. One of the most important parts of family communication is how well we listen to each other. The game we just played gives you a glimpse of how well you listen to and observe each other in your family. Some of you may have been surprised at how many questions you couldn't answer about your parents or preteens. Our goal today is to review principles for listening to each other."

Step 1

Begin with a brief review of the main points of this unit. (See the unit introduction for a summary of the main points of each session.) Involve some of your students by asking them to read the posters of the land mines and communication formulas. Then say, "Since we are talking about listening to each other, our class would like to give you, the parents, a little more detail about what we learned about being good listeners in our families."

Invite students to present part one of the "Are You Listening?" skit. Then say, "True listening is not just hearing words; it's understanding exactly what the other person meant to say to us. The father in the first skit *thought* he was listening. But he was so busy talking, he never let his daughter tell him what she really wanted to say. Let's ask our players to redo this scene and make the father a better listener." Have players present part two. Then say, "This is an example of listening that helps us build relationships in our families, but it's not easy for family members to listen to each other in this way. In our class, we looked at several principles from the Bible that helped us learn more about listening to each other."

Ask one of your students to read the first verse listed. Have that student also ask parents to suggest what the verse teaches about being good listeners and to write the responses on a

Materials
poster of the communication land mines and communication formulas from past sessions, photocopies of the skit from **Session 3** on page 34, Bible search chart from page 14 with only the references and headings written out, Bibles

poster (see page 14). Invite other students to do the same with the rest of the verses.

Conclude the review by saying, "The last verse, James 1:19, is a good verse to remember. Following the guidelines of this verse will unquestionably make us good listeners in our families."

Step 2

Say, "One of the most common problems in families is that the members don't take the time to really listen to each other. As a result, we never get to hear what is in the hearts of those who are closest to us, or learn what matters most to them. Having special times set aside for meaningful family conversations can help. Although we can't exactly program meaningful family conversations into our lives as we would a dentist appointment, in today's fast-paced world we often have to make time for sharing together. Family meals, bed time, or times set aside for talking can become strategic times for family sharing. But the success of family sharing times depends on our ability to listen to each other. Listening is a skill we learn best by doing. Let's spend some time listening to each other right now."

Divide participants into small groups. Be sure all the groups contain both adults and students, but for this exercise, be sure parents are in different groups than their preteens. This will give kids whose parents are not present an opportunity to feel included. When the groups have been formed, choose a volunteer to throw a dart at the bulletin board on which you have attached balloons containing the following questions. When a balloon is broken, have the dart thrower read the question aloud. Then allow several minutes for everyone to answer it within their small groups. Remind participants to refer to the biblical principles and formula for being a good listener. Then choose another volunteer and repeat the process. Continue until all balloons have been popped and all questions answered.

1. Parents, is there anything in your past you are ashamed of and wish you could change?

2. Kids, what are you most afraid will happen to you in your life?

3. Parents, what is your fondest memory from your childhood?

4. Kids, what do you most want your parents to do for you?

5. Parents, what is your greatest wish for your kids?

6. Kids, what would you like your family to do together more often?

Materials
balloons with questions inside of them, push pins or tape, bulletin board, darts

Step 3

Ask participants to sit together as families again. Distribute photocopies of the "Can We Talk?" handout and have everyone fill them out individually. When everyone is finished, ask families to compare their lists and develop a master list of subjects family members most indicated they want to talk about in future sharing times. Encourage parents to set a personal goal of initiating meaningful conversations around these subjects with their preteens in the future.

Materials
photocopies of page 48, pens or pencils

Take It to the Next Level

Say, "As we leave today, let's practice one other form of important family communication—giving and receiving affirmations. An affirmation is a verbal statement that communicates to other family members something you feel about them, appreciate about them, or positive qualities you see in them. Let's think of some examples." Guide the group to brainstorm many examples of affirmations. Write them on the board. Here are some suggestions:

1. I love your smile!
2. I'm really proud of you.
3. You are a great encourager.
4. I think you have a gift for drawing.
5. You're the best cook in the whole world!

Now ask family members to think of a personal affirmation they would like to give to the other members of their families. Allow time for everyone to affirm their family members. (Note: Kids without parents present can write down affirmations to give to family members, or can give affirmations to each other.)

Ask how it felt to receive this kind of message from others in their families. Encourage everyone to give affirmations as a regular part of their family's lives.

End your session with prayer, asking God to help each family strengthen their relationships by listening to each other.

Can We Talk?

Rate each statement below, using the following scale:

1 • I want to talk more to my parent/preteen about this subject.

2 • I want to talk less to my parent/preteen about this subject.

3 • I don't want to talk to my parent/preteen about this subject at all.

_____ Friends

_____ Something I'm afraid of

_____ Death (in general or someone who died)

_____ The future

_____ Help with homework

_____ Other things about school

_____ Our family's past history

_____ Problems parents are facing

_____ Questions about sex

_____ Something I'm worried about

_____ My Mom about my Dad

_____ My Dad about my Mom

_____ Why Mom _____

_____ Why Dad _____

_____ Other things I want to talk about more:

Overall, I rank our family's communication as:

_____ Terrific   _____ OK, but I wish it was better

_____ I'm happy the way it is   _____ We hardly communicate

One thing that would make communication in our family better is:

_____

_____

Peace Treaty

Scripture: Romans 12:18; James 1:19

Know all the basic concepts, key verses, and communication formulas presented throughout this unit and practice applying them.

Feel desirous to continue using good communication skills at home.

Incorporate at least one new communication skill into their home.

Part I: Drill Practice

Activity #1

Display all your posters from past sessions. Say, "We can think of good family communication as a battle we have to win. The enemy is poor communication that leads to misunderstandings, fights, and strained relationships with other family members. The land mines we studied are the weapons the enemy uses to destroy good communication in our families. We have to know these weapons well so we can see them coming and avoid using them." Have kids enthusiastically recite the communication land mines listed on your poster, which should read: Blaming, Harsh language, Broken promises, Responding in anger, Unclear messages, and Not listening. Say, "Our weapons are the communication formulas for giving clear messages, being a good listener, and minimizing family fights." Review each of these, having kids yell them several times.

Divide your class into teams of four kids each. Give each team a set of cards containing the land mines and formulas, one word per card, all mixed up. Take the posters down and instruct the teams to put their cards into the proper sequence. Conduct this as a race, awarding points to each team according to how they placed (i.e. if you have four teams, award forty points to the first place team, thirty points to second place, twenty to third, and ten to last place. As an option, instead of

Materials
posters of land mines and communication formulas from past sessions, land mines and formulas written out on cards (one word per card, one set per four students, jelly beans or *M&M's* candy, optional) chalkboard, chalk

points, award jelly beans or *M&M's* candy. Your kids may enjoy watching their pile of "points" grow.

Next, read the following situations. After each, ask one team to identify which land mine or formula the situation violates. If they are correct, award ten points; if incorrect, two points for trying. Then give all teams one minute to rewrite the situation, following the rules of good communication. Award five points to each team that completes a rewrite.

Situation #1

Mom: Joey, you spilled your milk again! Get the dish cloth and clean it up!

Joey: It's not my fault, Mom! If you hadn't filled the glass so full I wouldn't have spilled it! Why should I have to clean it up when it wasn't my fault?

Communication land mine: Blaming
Suggested Rewrite:

Joey: I'm sorry, Mom. I'll clean it up.

Situation #2

Dad: Maria, didn't you promise me you would do your chores right after supper? That was three hours ago, and they're still not done.

Maria: I guess I forgot.

Dad: Well, turn off the TV right now and go do them!

Maria: No! This is my favorite show! I'll do them before I go to bed. I promise!

Communication land mine: Broken promises; not doing what you say you will do.
Suggested Rewrite:

Maria: I'm sorry, Dad. I'll do them right now.

Situation #3

Mom: How's that math homework coming, Ryan?

Ryan: Math is the dumbest subject in the whole world! Who needs it, anyway?

Unclear message: What he said does not clearly express what he is feeling.

Clear message: Mom, will you please help me with this math problem? I can't figure it out.

Situation #4

Dad: I can't believe you're late again! I don't want to hear any of your stories, either! You're grounded for two weeks starting now!

Fran: That's unfair! You wouldn't do this to Christine if she came in late!

Not Listening: The father is not listening to his daughter.
Listening

Dad: You're late again! This can't continue.

Fran: I have a good reason this time! Would you just give me a minute to tell you what happened?

Dad: OK, but we're not leaving this room until we solve this problem. Deal?

Activity #2

Print the two key verses, Romans 12:18 and James 1:19, on a chalkboard. Say, "Winning the battle for good communication in our homes is hard work, but we have a secret weapon to help us—God's power. We can draw on God's power through prayer. We can also hide His commands in our hearts. Remembering these key verses can help us better communicate at home." Have kids read the verses aloud several times, erasing key words each time.

When the verses are completely erased, have class members stand in their teams so that the first person on each team is facing you, and the rest of the team is lined behind them. Then give the first word of one verse and ask the first person in line on the first team to say the second word. If he gets it right, award one point and have him move to the end of his team's line. If he misses, he still goes to the back of the line. Then point to the first person on the next team for the next word and do the same. Proceed until the verses have been stated correctly.

When the games are over, acknowledge the winning team. If you used edible points, let the teams eat their winnings.

Part 2: Application

For the "Dear Jockomo" skit, you or another adult will need to play Jockomo and have three kids play the parts of the studio audience. Jockomo is a talk show host who discusses letters from his listeners with his audience. Create the talk show environment by sitting on a tall stool and holding a microphone. Place your "audience" to your side so they can clearly see and hear. After you present the script, remain in character and invite the whole class to return the next week to participate in Jockomo's show.

To prepare for "next week's show," divide students into pairs and give each pair a photocopy of the "Dear Jockomo" letter from page 55. Allow five minutes for them to discuss the letter and think about how they could respond to Soccer Hater. Bring them back together again and choose one student to pretend to be the letter writer and read it to the "audience." Let kids

Materials
photocopies of pages 53-55, a high stool, a microphone, a stack of letter papers and envelopes, pens or pencils, paper, refreshments (optional)

offer their responses. Be prepared to help them by asking questions. After a few minutes of discussion, thank everyone for participating and invite them back to next week's show. Here are some suggestions to guide your discussion:

1. Biggest problem. Soccer Hater has not communicated with his parents about this issue. He is only guessing what they think about it, and he has not clearly communicated his feelings.

2. Send a clear message. He can tell them exactly how he feels, just as he did in the letter. He could even ask them to read his letter and then talk with them about it.

3. Listen to their feelings. As he communicates his feelings, he can also think about their point of view. Maybe he is a quitter, and they want to be sure he follows through with this activity before he starts another one. Maybe they see that he is really a good player and want to help him develop his skills. He needs to know what they are thinking and feeling before they move to the last step.

4. Work it out. After both sides have listened to each other, they can make a decision. If the parents insist he finish the season, he could ask that they not sign him up again next year. Maybe they would agree to let him start playing the trumpet after soccer, giving him something to look forward to throughout the soccer season.

Finally, divide the kids into pairs again. Distribute paper and pencils and ask them to write their own letter to Jockomo, expressing a family communication problem. This can be a real situation from their own lives or a made up one. Then return to the talk show format and invite several pairs to read their letters to the rest of the audience. Choose one letter and discuss it for several minutes, encouraging your students to incorporate as many of the principles of good communication as possible. Again, prompt the discussion by asking questions and suggesting a possible plan of action.

Close your session with a special prayer for all of your kids, asking God to help them strengthen their relationships at home through good communication skills. Pray for each student by name. If you like, give your kids a special treat as you close this unit.

Dear Jockomo

Jockomo: Welcome to "Dear Jockomo . . ." The show that offers advice to you—the listening audience. Just write me a letter stating your most pressing communication problem, and my audience and I will help you! Hey, let's give a hand to today's studio audience! *(applause, applause)*

Well, as you can see, the letters keep pouring in, and I've brought along a few for us to discuss today. *(Fumble with papers, spilling some on floor.)* Ah! Here's one I think our audience will find interesting.

Dear Jockomo,

I'm eleven years old and have an eight-year-old brother. Our mom works, and it's my job to watch my brother after school until she gets home. But my brother won't listen to me when I'm in charge. He says I'm bossy. I'm the big sister not the mother, so he doesn't have to do what I say. A couple of times he went to the park with his friends when I said he couldn't. Another time he had a friend over. They started messing around with matches and candles.

I'm really scared he's going to get hurt some day, and it will be all my fault. I tried talking to my mom about it, but she just sighs and says, "You two will have to work this out. I think you're old enough to handle it." How can I get my brother and my mom to listen to me?

Signed,

Scared

Jockomo: Scared has a real problem! How can we help?

Kid #1: If the kid won't listen, she should punch him out. That should make him pay attention!

Kid #2: Oh, right! Big help that would be! That would just make it worse!

Kid #3: I think she needs to tell her mom that she just won't baby-sit anymore. Let someone else take care of the brat!

Jockomo: Let me jump in here! First of all, let's think about what's really going on here. What's Scared's biggest problem?

Kid #2: Her younger brother won't do what she says.

Kid #1: No, that's not it! It's that no one is listening to her. Her brother doesn't take her seriously, and her mom won't help either.

Jockomo: You got it! Now, what advice can we give Scared to help her get her mom and brother to listen to her and understand how she really feels about this problem?

Kid #2: First, she needs to send a clear message to her brother. Maybe he thought she was only trying to boss him around and didn't know she was really scared.

Jockomo: Good idea! But what if he won't listen?

Kid #3: She could talk to him in a way that doesn't sound so bossy. *(Gets excited.)* Or, I know! How about if she asks him what he wants to do, and does it with him, you know, just until he sees that she's not just trying to boss him around.

All Kids: *Yes!*

Jockomo: What about the mom?

Kid #1: How about if she finds a different time to talk to her mom?

Kid #2: Yeah! My mom's really tired when she gets home from work, and I can't talk to her about anything. If I really need to talk to her, I wait until Saturday morning.

Kid #3: And if that doesn't work, Scared could write her a letter so she could say everything exactly the way she wants to and send a clear message!

Kid #1: But maybe she could still punch the kid's lights out and show him who's boss!

Kids #2 and #3: No way!

Kid #1: Just kidding!

Jockomo: Well, I see we're almost out of time. What last word of advice can we give our friend, Scared?

Kid #3: Find a way to send clear messages to your mom and brother . . .

Kid #1: . . . and choose actions that show your brother you want him to be safe. You're not just a bossy big sister!

Jockomo: Great! Well, that's all we have time for today! See you next week when I'll dip into my bag of letters again. Good-bye for now! *(Exit)*

Dear Jockomo,

My problem is that my parents signed me up for the soccer team again this fall, but I really hate playing soccer. I don't want to be on the team any more! My parents seem to think I love playing, and I think they think I should play because it's good for me or something. Anyway, I really want to take trumpet lessons! I just don't know how to ask my parents to let me quit soccer so I can do it.

Signed,
Soccer Hater

What is Soccer Hater's biggest problem?

_____

_____

_____

As a member of the studio audience, what advice would you give Soccer Hater:

Send a clear message to his parents

_____

_____

_____

Listen to their feelings

_____

_____

_____

Work it out

_____

_____

_____

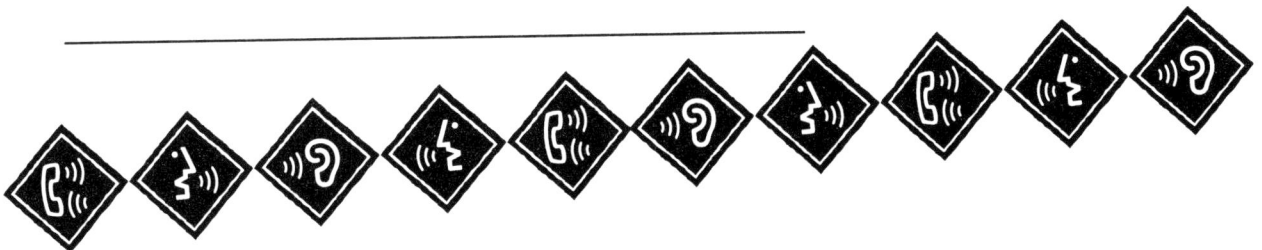

Unit 2

Flak Attack

Preteens live in a world where conflict is a fact of life. They encounter bullies, teasers, fake friends, and poor sports along with crude remarks, rumors, and vulgar language. In school, horseplay and teasing often escalate into threats and scuffles. Frequently, adolescents victimize each other. School and neighborhood violence is on the increase.

Violence in our society is increasing for many reasons. Adults are less available. Preteens are more isolated from parents and extended family members, and they are generally less connected to significant adults. They are not being taught constructive methods of conflict resolution. Their role models are action figures and TV villains who use violence to solve problems. Preteens are also less connected to their communities and churches.

Yet, our preteens want to learn to handle conflict. More importantly, they should desire to build life-long, healthy relationships with friends and family. Preteens need to learn how to forgive, how to cooperate and share, and how to be committed to others. They also need strong connections to positive social groups (family, friends, service groups, and church) and adult role models who resolve conflict positively.

This unit first explains and describes healthy relationships, then helps preteens develop specific skills in managing those relationships. These skills are strategies that help them prevent,

Session 1
Know four characteristics of healthy relationships.
Feel a desire to develop healthy relationships.
Identify healthy and unhealthy relationships.

Session 2
Know the power of words to create or reduce conflict.
Feel willing to control speech.
Use specific words and phrases to reduce conflict.

Session 3
Know good and poor methods of resolving conflicts.
Feel capable of using good methods to resolve conflicts.
Resolve conflicts in class situations and predict conflicts that may happen this week.

Session 4
Know a five-step process for resolving conflict.
Feel able to resolve conflicts.
Use appropriate strategies for specific conflicts.

reduce, and resolve conflict. The skills are taught in the context of how to manage healthy relationships.

Session 1 contrasts healthy and unhealthy relationships, helping students understand traits of healthy relationships. Habits used in healthy relationships help prevent conflict.

Session 2 emphasizes reducing conflicts that are inevitable between friends and enemies. The strategy is to use wise words to reduce conflict.

Session 3 teaches four general ways to resolve conflict: ignore the insult, walk away when you cannot change the other person's mind, reason with the person and discuss the problem, and take action to end the conflict.

Session 4 teaches students to get into the habit of thinking and praying before, during, and after the conflict. The goal of this session is to give students opportunities to rehearse strategies of resolving conflict, while reminding them to think and pray: whisper a prayer, stay calm, size up the situation, handle the conflict wisely, and pray for all those involved.

Using Puppets

Use two puppets in each session. Dress them in normal kid clothes with normal haircuts or hats. Make one friendly and the other unfriendly, and maintain these personalities for all four sessions.

In Session 1 the puppets help students discern differences between healthy and unhealthy relationships. In Session 2 the puppets help students learn wise words and phrases to use in conflicts. In Session 3 the puppets are used to role-play two friends—with one hurting the other. In Session 4 one puppet puts on a thinking cap and models the five-step process of thinking and praying through conflict while the other puppet refuses to wear the cap. Students review the results.

Let students role-play with the puppets and let the puppets become part of the class. Students may want to use the puppets with short skits they write in Sessions 3 and 4.

How Can I Make This Unit Successful?

Pray for your preteens and their friends. Recall times when you successfully resolved your conflicts with prayer, wise words, and habits of healthy relationships, such as forgiveness and grace. Be prepared to listen to your students. Ask the group to help find godly solutions to their real conflicts.

Devotion Guide

Week 1
Read what God says about healthy relationships
Monday	James 5:19, 20
Tuesday	Colossians 3:12-14
Wednesday	James 5:16
Thursday	1 Thessalonians 5:11, 18
Friday	Proverbs 27:17

Week 2
Read what God says about the words we use.
Monday	James 1:19
Tuesday	James 4:16
Wednesday	1 Timothy 4:12
Thursday	Proverbs 15:1
Friday	Ephesians 4:31, 32

Week 3
These devotions are offered on page 80. Read what God says about resolving conflicts.

Week 4
These devotions are offered on page 87. Read what God says about prayer when we have conflicts.

Who's on My Side?

Scripture: Proverbs 27:17

Know four characteristics of healthy relationships.

Feel a desire to develop healthy relationships.

Identify healthy and unhealthy relationships.

If students want to resolve their differences, they must learn to form healthy relationships with others and to recognize unhealthy relationships. This session focuses on conflict prevention and resolution. Students will learn four principles of forming healthy relationships. If these principles occur, conflict can be prevented or reduced. Students will evaluate their relationships and identify any unhealthy characteristics that may need to be changed.

Get Into the Game

To introduce today's topic, place a table in the center of the room and ask the group to gather around it. Select two students to arm wrestle. The winner takes on another person until someone else wins. The new winner challenges others. When several students have played, declare a winner. This situation may cause a conflict! If not, use the arm wrestling as an object lesson to define conflict. State that conflict occurs between people when one person wants one thing and the other person wants something else. Each person pushes to get his own way. Sometimes the conflict heats and people get angry. Sometimes conflict is so intense that friendships are broken. In the worst conflicts, people never reconcile and their friendship ends.

Ask if it is possible to have a friend with whom you never get into a conflict. Help students realize that even in the best of friendships, conflict will occur. What matters is how we handle it.

Describe three terms used in this unit: **Prevent conflict** (trying to avoid it when possible), **Reduce conflict** (trying to keep

Materials
table, chairs

a conflict from worsening), and **Resolve conflict** (coming to an understanding that takes away the conflict.)

State that God is the expert at handling conflict. God gives us principles or guidelines that can help us prevent, reduce, and resolve conflict. He is the great peacemaker. He invented healthy relationships. We want to discover God's principles of healthy relationships.

If you use puppets, introduce them and ask the class to name them. Use the puppets in any of the role-playing activities introduced in the four sessions.

Step 1

Activity #1

Display the two puppets. Tape one piece of construction paper on the wall above each puppet. Ask the class to name each puppet. State that these two puppets can teach us the difference between "good" or "healthy" relationships and "bad" or "unhealthy" relationships.

Introduce the first puppet as a close friend, someone we would want to spend time with or play with. Ask the students, "What words can you think of to describe this wonderful friend?" *(nice, kind)* Write a few responses on the paper next to this puppet.

Introduce the second puppet as someone we would consider as a bully or an enemy—someone who hurts us, disappoints us, or makes us mad. Ask, "What words can you think of to describe this bad friend?" *(mean, nasty)* Write a few responses on the sheet of paper next to this puppet.

Divide the class into two groups. Give one group the first puppet's sheet of construction paper and a marker. Give the second group the second puppet's sheet of construction paper and a marker. Ask both groups to think of other words that describe the good friend and the bad friend. Offer suggestions as needed.

Bring the groups back together. Tape the papers next to each puppet and read the lists.

Say, "Being a Christian means living in the real world. We will have conflicts with friends and enemies. We will find some friends who are easy to love. If we have healthy or good relationships with our friends, we can usually figure out the conflicts and solve them. We will also find bad friends who hurt us or disappoint us. If we try to have better relationships with our enemies, sometimes we can make enemies into friends!"

Materials
two kid puppets: one is friendly, the other looks mean; two pieces of construction paper; markers

Activity #2

This activity uses three Bible characters to compare healthy and unhealthy relationships. David and Jonathan's relationship is an example of a healthy relationship. David and King Saul's relationship is an example of an unhealthy relationship.

Divide the class into two smaller groups. Distribute page 66, pencils, and Bibles. Ask one group to study the relationship between David and Jonathan. Students need to read the Scripture references about Jonathan and David listed on the reproducible (1 Samuel 18:1-4; 20:1-4, 17-22, 35-42). Explain how Jonathan was a devoted friend to David. He was willing to give up being the next king because God had chosen David. Jonathan helped David by giving him his robe, armor, bow, and belt. By helping David escape from King Saul, Jonathan saved David's life. Ask the group to write down the ways Jonathan was a good friend to David and to be ready to share them with the other group.

1 Samuel 18:1-4—*Jonathan gave David his robe, armor, sword, bow, and belt.*

1 Samuel 20:1-4—*Jonathan tells David he will do whatever David needs to protect him from King Saul.*

1 Samuel 20:17-22—*Jonathan makes a plan to save David's life. He will shoot three arrows. Wherever the arrows land will tell David if he should stay or run for his life.*

1 Samuel 20:35-42—*Jonathan follows the plan and tells David good-bye.*

Ask the other group to study the relationship between David and King Saul, which occurs while Jonathan and David were best friends. Explain how God had chosen David to be the next king. Explain how King Saul was very jealous of David's deep, sincere love for God. To make the situation worse, King Saul was Jonathan's father. Jonathan was to be the next king. King Saul hated David because David was chosen to be the next king instead of Jonathan or any of King Saul's other sons. He felt threatened by David. King Saul shows the characteristics of an unhealthy relationship with David. Ask this group to read the Scripture references about King Saul and David from 1 Samuel (18:6-9, 15; 20:30-33). Ask the group to write the ways King Saul was an enemy to David, and to be ready to share them with the other group.

1 Samuel 18:6-9—*Saul was angry with David because he was very popular with the people and looked on him with suspicion.*

1 Samuel 18:10-15—*Saul threw a spear twice at David to kill him and was afraid of David because the Lord was with him. But Saul made David a commander of the army.*

1 Samuel 20:30-33—Saul vowed to kill David, and Saul was angry that Jonathan tried to help David.

Activity #3

Listen to the cassette recording or watch the video recording of preteens describing their best friends and worst enemies (the bullies). Talk about how we have both friends and enemies in life. God gives us the guidelines to handle conflicts with both friends and enemies, and asks us to love them. Ask students to play a guessing game with you. Ask students to guess four special words that help us get along with friends and make peace with enemies. These are the four characteristics of healthy relationships (respect, communication, commitment, and grace). Play a game similar to Hangman. Write enough blanks for the word "respect." Ask students to guess letters. If a letter is guessed but not found in the word "respect," draw the head of a stick figure. Students will eventually guess the correct letters. Repeat with the words "communication," "commitment," and "grace." Instead of drawing a gallows, noose, and a man hanging, draw stick figures with a head, stick body, two stick arms, and two stick legs. The more stick figures that are drawn, the more friends they will have if they can remember the four characteristics. The game does not end until all words are guessed with as many "friends" drawn as necessary.

After the four words are discovered, explain them briefly in Step 2.

Materials

a cassette or video recording of kids describing their best friends and their worst enemies (Note: Prepare the recording ahead of time or assign the small group to make a recording in the hall.), chalkboard, chalk

Step 2

Begin by explaining the four characteristics of healthy relationships to the class. If students can have these habits in their friendships, conflicts can actually be prevented. If students can try these ideas with their enemies, they may reduce or prevent conflicts and make friends.

Mutual respect is remembering to treat the other person as God's child.

Clear communication is listening to what the other person says and being able to understand it.

Commitment is being loyal to your friend, standing by him, and defending him.

Grace is forgiving him and giving him another chance.

If you used the puppets in Activity #1, ask students to tell you how the friendly puppet can show these characteristics to the mean puppet. Give an example of how the friendly puppet respects the mean puppet by remembering that the mean puppet is loved by God and God made him. Use the friendly puppet to listen to the mean puppet and repeat what the mean puppet has said. (If the mean puppet tells the friendly puppet why he is mad, the friendly puppet repeats it back to the mean puppet.) Use the friendly puppet to express loyalty ("I will help you and be your friend.") and to express grace ("I forgive you for hurting me.").

Students who studied the relationship of Jonathan and David may share how Jonathan was a good friend to David. Relate the four characteristics to these two friends. They respected each other, communicated clearly, and created a plan to save David. They vowed their commitment and displayed grace by accepting God's decision for David to be the next king.

Students who studied the relationship of David and King Saul may share how King Saul was an enemy toward David. Relate how King Saul failed in the four characteristics. He did not respect David, and he was jealous of him. King Saul sent mixed messages to David by trying to kill him and then making him captain over the army. King Saul was not committed to David. Rather, he tried to kill him many times. King Saul did not show grace to David.

Complete the story to show how David handled King Saul. David returned evil with good. He respected King Saul as God's anointed until God Himself removed Saul from being king. David sent Saul a message that he spared the king's life when he had the chance to kill him. David was committed to King Saul by playing music for him and for leading the army for the king. David showed the king grace by forgiving King Saul many times for trying to kill Him.

Step 3

Write one of the four characteristics on each sheet of construction paper: Respect, Communication, Commitment, and Grace. Place the red strips on the sheet labeled "Respect." Place the green strips on the sheet labeled "Communication." Place the yellow strips on the sheet labeled "Commitment." Place the orange strips on the sheet labeled "Grace."

Give each student a blank notecard and assign each student a verse from the following list. Each student will find the assigned verse and copy it onto the notecard. Students will then decide which of the four characteristics are described in the verse. Students will then glue the coordinating strips of paper to the backs of their notecards. Students will tape their verse cards on the wall as a visual to show how often the Bible mentions these four characteristics. Re-read the verses together as a group.

Materials
four large sheets of construction paper, notecards, pencils, glue sticks, several small strips of red, green, yellow, and orange paper

Philippians 4:6, 7 (communication, grace)
Colossians 3:12-14 (respect, grace)
James 5:19, 20 (communication, grace, respect)
1 Thessalonians 5:11 (communication)
2 Corinthians 1:3, 4 (grace)
1 Thessalonians 5:18 (respect, commitment)
James 5:16 (communication, grace)
Philippians 1:3 (respect)

Take It to the Next Level

Materials
photocopies of page 67, pencils

Lead students to discuss their relationships. What is the easiest characteristic of the four to have in friendship? What is the most difficult of the four characteristics to have in friendship? Ask students to think of specific friends or enemies. Which relationships have all four characteristics? Which relationships have only one or two characteristics?

Ask students to choose one friendship to check in this activity. Explain that they examine how healthy their friendships are by looking at the four characteristics of respect, communication, commitment, and grace.

Distribute photocopies of page 67 and pencils. Ask each student to think about one friendship. Rate each characteristic with a number from one to three. One means that this friendship does not have that characteristic at all. Three means this characteristic is very strong in this friendship. Ask students to add up the points.

20-21 pts. = a healthy relationship
17-19 pts. = a few areas need work
16 pts. or below = unhealthy relationship in some areas

Ask students how healthy their friendships are and what characteristic needs improvement. Then ask them to write that characteristic on the bottom of the page. The healthier the relationship, the more easily conflicts can be resolved.

Closing

Materials
paring knife or other knife, a blade sharpener

Summarize the session by explaining that every person we spend time with will be a friend or an enemy. Conflicts with both friends and enemies will happen. But the Bible shows us how to make the most of these conflicts. Read Proverbs 27:17. Say, "This verse talks about iron sharpening iron." Display the paring knife. "This knife is made of metal. How do we sharpen this knife when it gets dull?" Display the blade sharpener and demonstrate how to sharpen the knife blade. (*We use another piece of metal.)* "How does one person sharpen another?" *(People may have conflicts with us, but we can learn from the problems and become more like Jesus. Friends and enemies can help us be better people for the Lord.)* Close the session with prayer.

Snapshot of Two Relationships

The Relationship
Between Jonathan and David

Write down how Jonathan showed friendship to David.

1 Samuel 18:1-4 _____

_____

1 Samuel 20:1-4 _____

_____

1 Samuel 20:17-22 _____

_____

1 Samuel 20:35-42 _____

_____

The Relationship Between David and King Saul

Read the following Scriptures and write down
how King Saul was an enemy to David.

1 Samuel 18:6-9 _____

_____

1 Samuel 18:10-15 _____

_____

1 Samuel 20:30-33 _____

_____

David and Jonathan's relationship had these characteristics.

_____   _____   _____   _____

David and King Saul's relationship did not have these characteristics.
What opposite characteristics did this relationship have?

_____   _____   _____   _____

Survey of
Healthy and
Unhealthy Relationships

The relationship I am thinking about is with _____.

Does this person usually...
Circle a number:

lie?	• 1 • 2 • 3 •	or tell the truth?
think of self?	• 1 • 2 • 3 •	or think of others?
gang up on you along with a group?	• 1 • 2 • 3 •	or stand up for you against a group?
say rude words to you?	• 1 • 2 • 3 •	or say respectful words to you?
talk about himself/herself?	• 1 • 2 • 3 •	or listen to you?
hold grudges?	• 1 • 2 • 3 •	or forgive you?
ignore your opinion?	• 1 • 2 • 3 •	or care about your opinion?

Add up your score
Total points = _____

20-21 pts. = healthy relationship	17-19 pts. = a few areas need work	16 or below = unhealthy relationship in some areas

---

This week I will try to work on this relationship by _____

_____

_____

Keep Watch Over Your Words

Scriptures: Ephesians 4:31, 32;
Colossians 4:6; Timothy 4:12; Titus 3:2;
James 1:19; 3:2-10; 1 Peter 3:9-11
Memory Verse: Proverbs 15:1

Know the power of words to create or
reduce conflict.
Feel willing to control speech.
Use specific words and phrases to
reduce conflict.

Get Into the Game

Prior to the session, write the following lists onto separate
pieces of paper:
1. Horse's bit—tail, saddle, stirrups, reins, horseshoe
2. Ship's rudder—water, anchor, life preserver, steering
wheel, captain
3. Forest fire—trees, spark, flame, animals, smoke
Divide the class into three teams. Choose one person from
each team to be the captain. The first team's captain will come
forward and draw a slip of paper. He will then get one minute
to draw the words from the paper onto the chalkboard while
his teammates guess what he's drawing. The team will receive
one point for each correct answer and an extra point if the
main words are guessed (horse's bit, ship's rudder, forest fire).
The most points a team can earn is six. Do this until all three
teams have drawn. Then ask, "What do a horse's bit, a ship's
rudder, and a forest fire have in common? They can all be
found in James 3:2-6. James uses them to describe the tremen-
dous power of our words. Now we're going to learn more
about these three things."

Materials
three slips of paper with words listed on
them, chalkboard, chalk, timer or watch
with a second hand

Step 1

Activity #1

The students will examine the bit and bridle and will answer
the following questions about them. Students will need to be
ready to share their answers.
1. When the rider is in control of the bit, what can the rider
and horse do? List the types of walking, running, and tricks a
horse and rider can do. *(Horses can walk, sprint, cantor, gallop,*

Materials
model horse, saddle, bridle, bit (a Barbie
doll horse set or a real horse's bridle and
bit), a photo of a horse with a bit in its
mouth.

trot, stop, turn right or left, jump over fences and bars, round up cattle, pull a wagon or buggy, give rides to children, do show tricks, pull ploughs.)

2. When the rider is *not* in control of the reins which pull the bridle, what can happen to the horse, rider, and people and property in the way? *(bolt, throw a rider, break a leg or neck, trip and fall on a rider, run off a cliff, stampede, run blindly in a panic, trample people).*

3. How is a horse's bit like our tongue or the words we say? *(A bit in a horse's mouth is very small, but it directs a powerful animal. Our own mouths are very small, but they also direct our thoughts and actions. If we do not control our words, many people can be hurt.)*

4. How can gossip, lies, and rumors hurt people? *(Gossip is spreading information about people that is more untrue. Lies and rumors are also false information. These hurtful words cause people to be left out of the group or dropped as friends.)*

Activity #2

Read the paragraph on the sinking of the Titanic to the students and have them answer the following questions. Students need to be ready to share their answers.

Materials
picture of the Titanic or another great cruise ship, or a model of a great ship

The Titanic, the "unsinkable" ship, sailed on its maiden voyage on April 14-15, 1912. On its first trip from England, the Titanic's crew sighted an iceberg 1600 miles northeast of New York City. Before the ship could change course, it struck the iceberg. Lifeboats held less than half of the passengers. Only women and children were allowed to board. The ship sank in two and a half hours. Only 705 people survived, while 1,517 people died in the icy waters of the North Atlantic.

1. Where was the Titanic sailing? *(to New York City)*
2. What did the Titanic hit? *(an iceberg)*
3. How many people died as a result of the ship's sinking? *(1,517)*
4. How could the ship have avoided the iceberg? *(change its course)*

How are our words like the rudder of a great ship? *(The rudder on a great ship, like the Titanic, determines the direction the ship will go. Our words also determine the direction the argument will take. We can hit the iceberg head on by confronting someone with heated words. Or we can gently go around the iceberg by thinking of the best words to use at an appropriate time.)*

Activity #3

Distribute photocopies of page 73 and pencils. Have this group read the news story and answer the first set of questions.

Where did the fire take place? (5933 Cedarcreek, Winton Place)

When did the fire take place? (Sunday at 9:45 p.m.)

Who escaped the fire? (the parents and twin brothers)

Who did not escape the fire? (Becca)

How did the fire start? (the children were playing with matches)

What fueled the fire? (doesn't say)

How much damage did the fire do to the property and to the family? ($55,000 damage to home, loss of life to the family)

How is an argument like a fire? (It can get out of hand very easily and always destroys friendships. It can jump from one person to the next like a forest fire when people spread gossip, lies, and rumors.)

Ask students to use the same series of questions to think about a recent argument with a friend. Try to dig for the facts.

Where did the argument take place?

When did the argument take place?

Who won the argument?

Who lost the argument?

How did the argument get started?

What words kept the argument going and "fueled" the fire?

How much did the argument damage your friendship?

We need to use our words to put out fires by resolving hurt feelings. We need to avoid using our words to start fires. Careless words will cause untold damage to our friendships.

Step 2

Ask each group from the Step 1 activities to share their new knowledge about the horse's bit, the ship's rudder, and the fire. All three are powerful pictures of how the words we say can harm people if we do not control our words.

Display the friendly puppet and four signs containing the letters R, C, C, and G.

Let the puppet remind students that controlling our words is a big part of having healthy relationships. Have students name the characteristics the letters represent and brainstorm words that would show respect, clear communication, commitment, and grace.

Materials

photocopies of page 73, pencils

Materials

the friendly puppet from **Session 1**, four paper signs (each sign has one large letter on it: R, C, C, or G), stapler, 8" x 4" strips of construction paper, photocopies of page 74, pens or pencils

Distribute photocopies of page 74. As students think of phrases, they can write them down in their books. They will then cut out "pages" of the Word Watch book, assemble them in order, and staple it. Wise Words include the following:

1. Respect: Thank you, Please, and Excuse Me. I think your opinion is important. I appreciate you.

2. Clear Communication: What do you need? What do you think the problem is? Is this what you mean when you said . . . (mirror back what was said to show that you understand).

3. Commitment: How can we work this out? How can I help? I am listening. You can do it. We can work together.

4. Grace: I forgive you. Please, forgive me. We both were wrong. I was wrong. I am sorry.

Step 3

Materials
Bibles, list of verses

Ask students to sit in a circle on the floor with a Bible in their laps. Assign each student one of the following verses to locate and read silently: Proverbs 15:1; Ephesians 4:31, 32; 1 Timothy 4:12; Titus 3:2; James 1:19; James 4:16; 1 Peter 3:9; 1 Peter 3:10, 11. If there are more students than verses, start at the beginning of the list and assign the verses again. Encourage students to help each other find the verses and practice reading them quietly. Assist students who are having difficulty with particular words.

Each student will need to read and rehearse one verse. When students are ready, one begins by reading his verse. The next student reads his verse aloud, and so on. The idea is to be blitzed with Scriptures that are on the same topic.

When all students have read their verses around the circle, ask them what God wants them to do with their words. What guidelines does God give us concerning wise words? Two principles may emerge from your brief discussion: a gentle answer calms an angry person and words must always offer grace or forgiveness to others.

Take It to the Next Level

Divide students into pairs for this activity. Assign each pair one of the situations to role-play. The pair has to do the role play two ways. The first way uses bad attitudes and arguments to make the conflict worse. The second way uses wise words to resolve the conflict. Each skit is fifteen to twenty seconds long. Be available to offer suggestions as students plan their skits. Students may consult their word books for suggestions on words that may help their situations.

Common Conflicts

One person is using another friend's item (makeup, radio, earphones, soccer ball) and hasn't returned it yet.

One person has promised to call the friend, but has forgotten.

One person is not doing very well in a subject at school, and the other friend is doing great in that subject.

One person thinks it is fine to watch a certain movie, but the other friend is not allowed to watch the movie.

One person tells a lie about someone else to a friend.

One person hurts his friend's feelings and does not realize it.

One person makes fun of a person with a disability.

One person gets some special school or team recognition (a trophy or special part in a play) and the other friend does not.

Close the session with prayer. Ask God to help your students use appropriate words to reduce and resolve conflicts with friends and enemies.

The Youthful Times

VOL. CXLVI...No. 50,123   SUNDAY   ONE DOLLAR

Matches claim child's life

Next level staff report

One child died in a fire at 5933 Cedarcreek Sunday when she and her siblings set the house ablaze by playing with matches.

Five-year-old Becca Johnson was pronounced dead at Children's Hospital due to smoke inhalation. She and her twin brothers, seven-year-old Wayne and Aaron Johnson had been playing with matches in her second-story bedroom when the fire began. The two children, along with their parents, Jack and Karen Johnson, were rescued from a second-story window by firefighters.

The one-alarm fire at 9:45 p.m. that brought twenty firefighters to the Winton Place home was estimated at $55,000 loss.

Read the news story and answer these questions.

Where did the fire take place?

_____
_____
_____

When did the fire take place?

_____
_____
_____

Who escaped the fire? _____

_____
_____
_____

Who did not escape the fire? _____

_____
_____
_____

How did the fire start? _____

_____
_____
_____

What fueled the fire? _____

_____
_____
_____

How much damage did the fire do to the property and to the family?

_____
_____
_____

How is an argument like a fire?

_____
_____
_____

Use the same series of questions to think about a recent argument with a friend.

Where did the argument take place?

_____
_____
_____

When did the argument take place?

_____
_____
_____

Who won the argument? _____

_____
_____
_____

Who lost the argument? _____

_____
_____
_____

How did the argument get started?

_____
_____
_____

What words kept the argument going and "fueled" the fire?

_____
_____
_____

How much damage did the argument do to your friendship?

_____
_____
_____

"Let your conversation be always full of grace, seasoned with salt..."
(Colossians 4:6).

"A gentle answer turns away wrath, but a harsh word stirs up anger"
(Proverbs 15:1).

Word Watch Book

I will show respect for others by saying

_____
_____
_____
_____
_____
_____
_____

Philippians 1:3, 4

I will use clear communication by saying

_____
_____
_____
_____
_____
_____
_____

James 5:19, 20

I will show commitment by saying

_____
_____
_____
_____
_____
_____
_____

1 Thessalonians 5:11, 18

I will give grace by saying

_____
_____
_____
_____
_____
_____
_____

James 5:16; Philippians 1:3

Battle Plans

Scriptures: Luke 6:27-31; Matthew 13:53-58; 22:34-46; Mark 11:15-17

Memory Verse: 2 Timothy 1:7

Know good and poor methods of resolving conflicts.

Feel capable of using good methods to resolve conflicts.

Resolve conflicts in class situations and predict conflicts that may happen this week.

Get Into the Game

Conflicts are inevitable! They will occur between friends and enemies. We can sometimes prevent conflicts by working harder at healthy relationships. We can reduce conflicts by using wise words in a gentle voice. But sometimes conflicts are unavoidable! To avoid physical violence, we need to have a battle plan. Thinking ahead helps us handle conflict in positive ways.

Ask for volunteers to play a game. Take four volunteers into the hall and ask them to do an action move for the class. Ask one student to walk in and do a karate chop. Ask another student to do fake punches in the air. Ask the next student to give a championship wrestling elbow jab on the floor. Ask the fourth student to do a spin around karate kick. After the four students have done their actions, ask the class what these four actions have in common. (*They are all ways to fail when it comes to resolving conflict.*)

Discuss these moves as common ways people fight. Fighting hand to hand is one of the worst ways to resolve conflict. Physical violence is also the only way some kids know how to resolve conflict. If someone attacks, you have a right to defend yourself, but you never have the right to throw the first punch! There are better ways to resolve conflict.

Step 1

Activity #1

Instruct students that some Bible characters are good examples of resolving conflict. We can learn appropriate ways to handle conflict from them. The very same people sometimes

Materials
photocopies of page 79

failed by handling conflict in poor ways.

Ask the students preparing this activity to read the monologues on page 79 and decide which students will role-play or read the six situations. Three of the situations demonstrate poor ways to handle conflict. The other three situations demonstrate positive ways to handle conflict. There are two situations for each biblical character, a good method and a bad method for handling conflict. Suggestion: Have the same student read both situations for Moses, another student read both situations for Joseph, and so on. Convey the idea that people can make both poor and good choices.

Activity #2

Read the following situation and discuss the possible ways to resolve the conflict. Ask students to think of as many different ways as possible for Chad and Larry to resolve the conflict. Ask students to use the puppets to role-play each possibility. Check with the group. Ask what strategies they have thought of and suggest the four strategies in the lesson: **ignore, walk away, reason, and take action.**

Chad and Larry had been best friends since kindergarten. Chad learned that he had to move to another state. Chad did not want to say good-bye to Larry. The whole week before Chad moved, he would not talk to Larry. Larry thought Chad was mad at him and did not want to be friends anymore. How will Larry try to resolve this conflict?

Ask a volunteer to role-play the situation by ignoring Chad. Ask another volunteer to role-play a different ending by walking away from Chad's house. Ask another volunteer to role-play a third way by reasoning or discussing the problem with Chad. Ask the last volunteer to role-play another ending by confronting Chad and telling him how much he has hurt Larry.

Activity #3

Give this group four Scripture passages: Luke 6:27-31; Matthew 13:53-58; Matthew 22:34-46; Mark 11:15-17. Ask students to read the passages. If they are not familiar with the story backgrounds, explain what is happening in each situation and answer questions. Ask students to describe how Jesus resolved the conflicts in these four situations. Students should be prepared to share their information.

1. Luke 6:27-31. Jesus teaches us to turn the other cheek, ignore the insult, and give back something good when we have been hurt. Jesus often ignored insults and continued His work.

2. Matthew 13:53-58. Jesus walked away from His home-

Materials
two puppets

Materials
poster board, Bibles, and markers

town because He knew the people would not change their minds and believe in Him.

3. Matthew 22:34-46. Jesus reasoned with the Pharisees who challenged Him. He also used these debates as a time to teach people the truth of the law and expose the distortions made by the Pharisees.

4. Mark 11:15-17. Jesus turned over the tables of the money changers in the temple. He took action against evil.

Step 2

Ask students who have prepared monologues from Activity #1 to line up in the front of the room.

Introduce the monologues as Bible characters who sometimes handled conflicts very well, but at other times handled conflicts poorly. As each monologue is given, ask students to decide if the character handled the conflict well or poorly, and *why* they think that. Allow disagreements. Give students an opportunity to resolve these "conflicts" by reasoning with each other. Ask students to explain their reasons. (Note: The odd-numbered monologues display poor ways to resolve conflict. The even-numbered monologues display good ways to resolve conflict.)

Lying, hitting, and breaking God's laws are bad ways to resolve conflict. Following God's plan, confronting people when they are wrong, and forgiving people are good examples of resolving conflict appropriately.

Tell students that Jesus teaches us four very helpful ways to resolve conflict. Ask students from Activity #3 to present the information they discovered about how Jesus resolved conflict.

Step 3

Give students an opportunity to create posters of conflict resolution ideas. They may use the four ideas from Jesus' life (ignore, walk away, reason, and take action), or brainstorm other ways to resolve conflicts. The posters will be used in **Session 4** as students determine how to resolve current conflicts.

Students may brainstorm these good ideas: remember to work on their relationships, use wise words, forgive, don't lie or spread rumors, don't seek revenge, go directly to the person and ask if the rumor is true.

Materials
poster board, markers

Take It to the Next Level

Read the following situations and discuss possible ways to resolve the conflicts. Refer to the posters. Usually, the conflict can be resolved in several ways. Some choices may be wiser than others in each situation. Discuss which choices are good, better, and best by asking which choices help or hurt friend-ships.

1. At school I was walking down the hallway and was hit by a heavy backpack. The kid was a year older than me and laughed.

2. Kids at the next table in the school cafeteria were laughing about my art project on display in the library.

3. My friend told me she was sick and couldn't spend the night at my house, but she went roller skating with another friend instead.

Distribute photocopies of page 80. Predict any conflicts that may come up during the next week. Describe the devotional Scripture verses. Ask students to use this guide during the week. Tell them to write down any conflicts that happen and how they resolved them or plan to resolve them. (Note: The conflict resolution for any particular day may not necessarily come from that day's Scripture.)

Close with prayer for wisdom in choosing how to resolve the conflicts that occur during the next week.

Materials
photocopies of page 80

Bible Show and Tell

1. I am Abraham. God has been leading me to a land of promise. Along the way, I encountered a powerful king. To keep peace with the king, I lied to him about my beautiful wife Sarah. I told him that Sarah was my sister and gave her to him as his wife. I lied so he would not kill me and take Sarah from me.

2. I am Abraham. My nephew Lot and I needed to separate our herds on different lands because our shepherds were fighting. There was great land near the city and much poorer land along the mountains. Instead of fighting with Lot, I let him choose the land he wanted. He chose the best land by the city.

3. I am Joseph. My brothers hated me because I gave my father a bad report about them. I also told them about my dreams. They beat me and threw me into a deep well. Then they sold me to Egyptian slave traders.

4. I am Joseph. I became a rich and powerful leader in Egypt. I had the power to kill my brothers who came to Egypt to buy grain during a famine. But I forgave them for beating me and selling me to the Egyptians.

5. I am Moses. Before being chosen by God to speak to Pharaoh, I saw a Hebrew beaten by an Egyptian. No one was around so I killed the Egyptian and hid him. When others found out what I had done, I ran away.

6. I am Moses. When I came down the mountain with the Ten Commandments, I saw the Hebrew people dancing around an idol. I confronted them and told them they were wicked. I burned the idol and ground it into fine dust. I added the dust to the water and made them drink it. God also punished the Hebrews for worshiping the false god.

Weekly Devotion Guide and Journal

Day and Verse	Conflict	How I Resolved It
Monday **Read Proverbs 18:15**		
Tuesday **Read Colossians 3:12-14**		
Wednesday **Read James 1:19**		
Thursday **Read 1 Peter 3:9**		
Friday **Read 1 Timothy 4:12**		
Saturday **Read Colossians 4:6**		
Sunday **Read Philippians 1:3**		

The Battle Is On!

Scripture: Matthew 13:53-58; 22:34-46; Mark 11:15-17; Luke 6:27-31; 2 Timothy 1:7
Memory Verse: Philippians 4:6, 7

Know a five-step process for resolving conflict.
Feel able to resolve conflicts.
Use appropriate strategies for specific conflicts.

Get Into the Game

Use this activity to review the concepts in Sessions 1, 2, and 3. Ask students to define conflict (two people want different things so they disagree), who we have conflict with (friends and enemies), what good characteristics are developed in healthy relationships (respect, clear communication, commitment, and grace).

Describe a personal situation in which you did all you could do to avoid conflict, but conflict occurred anyway. When we cannot avoid conflict, we need to make plans to resolve it.

Ask students to make a strategy bag to help them resolve conflicts. The four strategies are modeled by Jesus. Refer to posters made last week (ignore the insult, walk away if you cannot change their minds, reason or compromise, take action to end the conflict). Ask students to list other strategies that can help resolve conflict (laugh at ourselves, ask forgiveness, set a time to talk later when we're not mad, ask a trusted adult for help, write a letter to the person, make a phone call).

Distribute paper bags, blank notecards, and markers. Ask students to write one strategy on each notecard and put the notecards in the bag. Have students write their names on their bags.

Materials
paper bags, notecards, markers (one of each per student)

Step 1

Activity #1

This group will read Philippians 4:6, 7. The group will make up motions or actions for the words in the verses to help them memorize the passage. Then the group will rehearse the motions and lead the class in reciting the verses. Suggested motions follow:

"do not be anxious"	hands that are shaking
"about anything"	one hand facing down, moves away from body
"but in everything"	two hands facing up to receive
"by prayer and petition"	two hands together praying
"with thanksgiving"	heads bowed
"present your requests"	two hands giving away
"to God"	point upward
"and the peace of God"	cross hands over heart
"which transcends"	hand over head like it's "over our heads"
"all understanding"	point to brain
"will guard your hearts"	cross hands over heart
"and minds"	two hands on head
"in Christ Jesus"	point upward

Discuss what the verse means. Ask students to say it in their own words. Say, "When we face conflict, what attitudes do we need to have?" *(Don't be anxious, but be thankful, expect peace, trust Jesus to help, don't expect to understand the conflict or the way God works it out.)* "What will God do in conflicts?" *(He will guard our hearts and minds, give us peace, help us do the best thing.)*

Activity #2

Prepare the following role plays. In each role play, both people will disagree until they are mad, then the action will freeze. The students will use their strategy bags to find the best way to resolve the problem. Students will pull out the strategy they believe to be the best. If students disagree, ask them to explain why they think their strategy would work best.

1. Two students are working together to write a play for school. One person wants to end the play with a happy ending. The other wants to end the play with a tragic ending.

2. Two friends have parents who are also friends. The families went on vacation together and will no longer speak to each other because of problems on the trip. The two friends each think the other friend's parents were to blame. One set of parents forgot to make enough reservations for the other family and cost the other family extra money. The other set of parents did not service their van and had two flat tires, which caused the group to miss a planned activity.

3. One friend told her best friend about a family problem. The next day the best friend gossiped about the problem to a group of other friends. The first friend had told her best friend not to tell anyone, but her best friend broke that trust.

Materials
strategy bags, role-play list

Activity #3

Use the puppets from the first two sessions and two baseball caps that fit them. Model this activity with the puppets, then let each student make a thinking cap to take home. Write the five steps of thinking and praying through conflict on a notecard: whisper a prayer, stay calm, size up the situation, handle the conflict wisely, and pray for all involved after the conflict is over. Tape the card to the front of the baseball cap so the card is visible to students. On the other baseball cap, tape a note-card that says, "Say what I want . . . Do what I want . . . Hurt anyone I want . . . Don't think! . . . Don't Pray!" Put the first baseball cap on the friendly puppet and the second baseball cap backwards on the mean puppet.

Ask the group to discuss the consequences of handling conflict using the five steps of thinking and praying as compared to handling conflict by just reacting. Have the group write a short puppet skit that shows the first puppet using the five steps of thinking and praying through conflict. Ask the group to write another short puppet skit that shows the mean puppet saying and doing anything he wants without thinking or praying.

Suggestions for Skits

1. One puppet has loaned a much-loved item to a friend, and the friend will not return the item.

2. One puppet planned to go to a school activity with another friend, and the friend canceled.

3. One puppet asked a friend to come to church, and the friend told him to forget it.

4. One puppet thinks everyone at school makes fun of him.

Follow-up the skits by giving the mean puppet the thinking cap. Replay the skit as if the puppet was using the five steps of thinking and praying through conflicts. Notice the differences as the mean puppet learns to think and pray before, during, and after conflict.

Step 2

Present the Philippians 4:6, 7 passage with motions. Describe the attitudes and actions this verse asks us to have during conflict. This is an attitude check.

Say, "Because we are Christians, we have access to God's help. But we have to think and pray to prepare ourselves for the conflict. If we do not think and pray first, the conflict usually turns into a big mess. However, if we think and pray first, we can handle the conflict in the best way possible." Offer a personal account of not praying before a conflict and the

Materials
old baseball or football caps (one per student), scissors, safety pins, puppets, paper, pens or pencils

Materials
photocopies of page 86, pencils

negative result. Offer a contrasting account of praying before a conflict and the positive result.

Say, "Make these decisions to prepare yourself for the conflict and to invite the Lord to help you. Don't go into a conflict cold!" Distribute photocopies of page 86 and instruct students on the thinking and praying processes that invite the Lord to help when we try to resolve conflict:

1. Whisper a prayer that this problem can be worked out.
2. Remind yourself to stay calm and speak calmly.
3. Evaluate the situation. Ask these questions: "Can I ignore this? Will they quit if I ignore them? Is it worth fighting about? Will I change their minds? If not, can I walk away and simply not fight about it? Is this something I need to discuss, reason, or compromise about? Can I make peace? Do I need to take some action?"
4. Choose a strategy to handle the conflict.
5. Pray for yourself and for the other person.

Ask the group who wrote the two puppet skits to perform the skits. Ask students if they could tell which puppet used God's plan for thinking and praying through conflict and which puppet did not think or pray. Ask students to describe the consequences for each puppet. What will happen to the puppet who used good thinking and praying? What will happen to the puppet who did not think and pray?

Have students complete the reproducible page at this time.

Step 3

Instruct students on the importance of prayer to resolve conflict. It always changes how the conflict turns out. Students who completed role plays in Activity #2 may present them now. Ask other students to use their strategy bags to decide how the players could best resolve the situations. If students made thinking caps, ask them to wear their thinking caps during this activity to practice thinking during conflicts.

Each conflict will be presented until the action freezes. When the action stops each time, remind students to think of what they would do if they were in that situation. Remind them to whisper a prayer, calm down, and then evaluate whether to walk away or confront. Ask students to choose a strategy out of their bags that would make the most sense. Give students an opportunity to hold up their cards from their strategy bags. Have students explain why this strategy would work best to resolve the conflict. If students disagree, ask them to explain their reasons. After the group decides which strategy would work best, remind them of the final step to resolving conflict: pray for yourself and the other person.

Take It to the Next Level

Materials
photocopies of page 87, Bibles, pencils

Challenge students to experiment with resolving conflicts this week. Distribute photocopies of page 87. This page is almost identical to the journal page from last week, except the devotional passages are different.

Ask students to think about the kinds of conflicts that usually happen on specific days (e.g., Thursday is gym class, and one kid always teases me because he runs faster than I do.) Ask them if any unusual events are planned for this week. What conflicts may occur because of these unusual events? Instruct students to write a phrase in the first column next to that day which notes the potential conflict. Ask students to also write possible ways to resolve the conflict in the second column.

Pray with the class about conflicts that may occur during the week. Remind them of Philippians 4:6, 7 and godly attitudes toward conflict. Remind them to use their strategy bags and thinking caps to think and pray before, during, and after conflicts. Ask students to complete the journal and devotion guide by reading the passage in the morning and filling in any notes about conflicts or how conflicts were resolved during the day.

Thinking and Praying Through Conflicts

Fill in the blanks, then discuss them with your group.

_____ a prayer.
"Dear Father, this situation is getting out of hand. Help us both to keep our heads and talk this out."

_____ calm.
Keep a calm voice and say gentle words. Think clearly.

_____ the situation.
"Are they listening to me? Can I change their minds? Maybe I should just walk away or ignore them. Are they willing to discuss it calmly? Do I need to confront this person? Do I need to take action against this person for his own good?"

_____ the conflict wisely.

Use the strategies you have learned:

Ignore the insult.
Walk away if the people will not listen.
Reason or discuss the situation. Compromise and negotiate to find a reasonable solution.
Take action by going to a caring adult or parent about the problem.

Others: _____

_____

_____ again for yourself and for the other person involved in the conflict.

Write about one time when you had a conflict with a friend or enemy.

How did you try to resolve your conflict?

How could you have handled the conflict another way?

Devotion Guide and Conflict Journal

Day and Verse	Conflict	How I Resolved It
Monday Read Matthew 18:15-17		
Tuesday Read Matthew 18:21-35		
Wednesday Read Matthew 13:53-58		
Thursday Read Matthew 12:36, 37		
Friday Read Matthew 5:38-42		
Saturday Read Matthew 5:43-48		
Sunday Read Matthew 5:10-12		

Think about one particular conflict you had this week.

Did you remember to whisper a prayer before your conflict?
Did you remember to stay calm ?
Did you size up the situation?
Did you handle the conflict wisely?
Did you pray for all of the people involved in the conflict after it was over?

How was the outcome different because you were thinking and praying?

Family Feud

Plan a group party for students and their families and friends as the last session in the series. Your students will enjoy laughing and joking about typical feuds they experience while they play a version of the former gameshow, Family Feud.

The session is designed to be lighthearted and fun while reinforcing the principles and strategies of conflict resolution discovered in Sessions 1 through 4. To prepare for the Family Feud game, students could prepare a large sign similar to the game show. Students could also help write the conflict situations that will be presented as questions in the game. Write ten to fifteen situations. Some examples are given on pages 91 and 92, but modify any situations and write new situations that may better apply to your group. For each situation, write three possible ways to resolve the conflict. If you list them, the first resolution is worth three points, the second is worth two points, and the third is worth one point. Write them on transparencies, and reveal them as they are guessed by the teams during the game. Make sure everyone can see the answers. Reveal only the answers that are given by the team during the game. Use as many situations as possible to fill a half hour of time.

The game can be set up easily. To play, each family or friend group needs to choose five team players. Each team will have a chance to play at least one time. Set up rounds:

Team A plays Team B in round 1.
Team C plays Team D in round 2.
Team E plays Team F in round 3.

After teams are formed and assigned to rounds, play is ready to begin. Read one situation to both teams. Each player on the first team offers a different way to resolve the conflict. The phrases are checked against a list on the overhead and marked if they are close enough to match. The players will offer many good ways to resolve the situation, but they will score points if they say one of the three answers written on the overhead transparency. The points for each correct answer are counted for the first team. The second team may either finish guessing the items that were not guessed, or they may try a new situation. The second team needs to make more points than the first team.

The team with the most points wins the round. If teams tie, read a new situation and ask each team to give their best answer. The answers need to show up on the transparency list. The answer with the most points wins the round.

Conclude the game by thanking the teams for their participation and cooperation. Remind them that they are all winners if they can think and pray while resolving their conflicts wisely! Offer a brief devotion summarizing the unit. Use the Scripture passage in Jesus' great Sermon on the Mount (Matthew 5) that describes friends and enemies. Say, "In Matthew 5:43-48 Jesus teaches us to not only love our friends, but we are also to love our enemies and pray for them. When we experience conflict with friends or enemies, we must handle the conflict with prayer and resolve the conflict fairly and lovingly. We must be ready to forgive and offer grace."

Suggestions for Preparing the Transparencies

1. Write the conflict situation in a brief sentence. Write the first way to resolve the conflict. Put a number (30) beside it. Write the second way to resolve the conflict. Put a number (20) beside it. Write the third way to resolve the conflict. Put a number (10) beside it.

2. Write ten to fifteen conflict situations and three good ways to resolve the conflicts.

3. Copy them in a machine that makes transparencies and then make two additional paper copies of the questions.

4. Give one paper copy to the "host" of the game show.

Use the other paper copy to cover the transparency, so the light cannot project them on the wall. Cut out each sentence as a strip of paper. Tape it over the identical sentence on the transparency. Make sure the words on the paper strips are facing up. The paper words will be covering the same transparency words (so you will know what words are under the strips). When the teams give their answers, read the paper strips. If the answer is listed, uncover it so the transparency words will show on the wall. If you tape only one end of the strip to the transparency, flip it to reveal the words underneath.

Examples of Conflict Situations and Possible Resolutions

1. Jeff tried to sell magazine subscriptions for the school PTA to his neighbors, but he did not have much luck. His friend Todd had already taken orders on Jeff's street. Todd had promised to give Jeff a chance first. Both boys wanted the prize for selling the most.

30 – Jeff should just go to another street and sell magazine subscriptions.

20 – Jeff should make a plan to work together with Todd to cover the whole town, and the one who wins will share the prize with the other boy.

10 – Jeff should call Todd and point out that Todd broke a promise just to beat him at sales.

2. Melinda wanted to be the most popular girl in her class. She ignored all the other girls who did not wear makeup and designer clothes. She even ignored her best friend, Tonya.

30 – Tonya should call Melinda and talk to her about being a snob.

20 – Tonya should ignore Melinda and find other friends.

10 – Tonya should wait until Melinda's snobbiness causes Melinda to have no friends at all. Then Tonya should discuss what went wrong and, as a true friend, forgive Melinda.

3. Nick always teases his best friend, Tony's, little brother by calling him names and tripping him.

30 – Tony should take action and tell an adult.

20 – Tony should reason with Nick and tell him not to tease his brother.

10 – Tony should tell his little brother to tell a parent when Nick teases him.

4. Some kids cut in line at Spider Mountain, the new roller coaster at the amusement park.

30 – Tell an adult or worker at the park.

20 – Avoid the line jumpers.

10 – Cut in front of them the next time you see them.

5. Jenny thought Carla was her best friend until Carla moved. Carla's new house is in a neighborhood on the other side of town. Now Carla never returns Jenny's phone calls.

30 – Jenny could write Carla a letter.

20 – Jenny could ask other friends if Carla is OK.

10 – Jenny could find other friends.

6. At the bus stop all the kids noticed Tasha's new neon green, high-top gym shoes. Randy made a cruel remark about aliens landing on their street. All the kids laughed at Tasha.

30 – Tasha could ignore the insult.

20 – Tasha could tell them how much it hurts to be laughed at.

10 – Tasha could stop wearing her shoes to school.

7. Midge and Stephanie were best friends. When they were placed on different soccer teams, they became bitter rivals. Midge's team beat Stephanie's team twice. Stephanie began to hate Midge and act like a poor sport.

30 – Midge could wait until after the season, and then try to talk to Stephanie.

20 – Midge could invite Stephanie over to practice together.

10 – Midge could ignore Stephanie's insults.

8. Carrie's parents divorced, and Carrie now travels on weekends to visit her father. Carrie overheard one of her friends say that her dad is sick in a hospital far away, and Carrie visits him there each weekend.

30 – Carrie could tell her friend not to tell others about her weekends.

20 – Carrie could tell her friends about her new living arrangements.

10 – Carrie could make friends with other kids who have the same circumstances.

9. After Marvin won the science fair, he bragged to his classmates that he was the next Mr. Wizard.

30 – Ignore the boasting.

20 – Remind Marvin that the greatest scientist is God.

10 – Congratulate Marvin for his great achievement and be happy for him.

10. The neighbors' dog barks day and night. No one can sleep at your house.

30 – Kindly tell your neighbor how the dog is affecting your family.

20 – Ask the owners to check the dog's health. (It may be hungry or need a distemper shot.)

10 – Call the police and report the dog.

11. Whatever Ken borrows, he brings back late and usually it is broken.

30 – Do not loan items to Ken any more.

20 – Ask Ken to replace the items he broke.

10 – If Ken needs an item, suggest other items he could use instead.

12. The first time Rayna saw her neighbor, he kicked over his new bike. She decided she did not like him and never would.

30 – Rayna could watch him and see if he displays any more destructive behavior.

20 – Rayna should avoid playing with him if he hits or kicks items regularly.

10 – Rayna should tell her parents about him.

13. Mark and Colleen voted in the mock presidential election at their school. They voted for different candidates and argued about the issues at lunch.

30 – If they cannot persuade each other, they should walk away from the argument (agree to disagree).

20 – Colleen and Mark could discuss what they do agree on.

10 – Colleen and Mark could do more research on the issues and talk to others to get better information.

14. Jerry sits beside Marty, a visually impaired student in his class. Jerry noticed that often the teacher forgets about Marty's special needs. Sometimes Marty is upset, but he doesn't say anything.

30 – Jerry could encourage Marty to tell the teacher he needs help.

20 – Jerry could tell the teacher Marty needs help.

10 – Jerry could offer to be Marty's study buddy.

15. Ben was short compared to other kids his age. Some kids called him Shrimp.

30 – Ben could discover famous, successful people who were also short.

20 – Ben could find ways to be good at things that do not require him to be tall.

10 – Ben could ignore the insults.

Peace Patrol

Get Into the Game

Conflicts occur because we are human. Even when we work together to help others, conflicts arise. Some of us are late, while others are always prompt. Because we are human, we often agree on the end result, but each person has a different plan. The ideas clash, and we argue instead of working. Because we are human, our egos need to be stroked, or we have to please everyone. Some of us are so stubborn, we cannot say we are sorry or forgive others.

These are common conflicts that occur when groups get together to do projects. They occur in elders' meetings and benevolence committee meetings, as well as in youth groups and Sunday school classes. These settings can be wonderful opportunities for preteens to watch and learn as adults positively resolve conflict. They also can be great working object lessons for our students to practice strategies of resolving conflict and develop habits of building healthy relationships. Service projects also help preteens strengthen their connections with the community.

In this session, students will work together on a project. Ask all students to join you in the "peace patrol," an elite corps of people who want to create peace out of conflict. They are dedicated to helping others pray and think through conflict. The goal is to bring God's peace into tense situations.

Materials
"deputy" badges or adhesive labels for a hat that says, "Peace Patrol" for each student

Before this session, announce the service project. Enlist help from parents. Inform the people who will be helped, and ask them to help plan. Communicate the information to your students' parents. Prepare materials to have available during this session. The primary goal of the session is to give students an opportunity to reinforce conflict resolution strategies and to develop stronger habits of good relationships. This is on-the-job training.

Step 1

Select one street in your city or town to be cleaned. Call city council or the chamber of commerce for information and for permission to clean the street. Provide garbage bags, recycled cardboard boxes, rubber gloves, and cold pop or hot chocolate (depending on the weather). Set the time and the meeting place. Send a note to parents asking permission. Announce the cleanup date in the church paper or youth newsletter. Gather supplies. Ask people to bring rakes or heavy garden gloves (if leaves and debris need to be cleaned). You may also want to bring window cleaning supplies for store windows.

Step 2

On the day of the project, gather helpers. Before the work starts, go over each person's jobs and their allotted time to complete the job. Give each helper the supplies needed for the cleanup.

Step 3

Before you dismiss the group to work, give them the badge or hat with the sticker. Encourage them to be on the "Peace Patrol" as they work—to work together, to talk about problems or differences of opinion, to help others resolve any conflicts during the cleanup. Also encourage them to have fun!

Take it to the Next Level

At the conclusion of the cleanup, distribute cold pop or hot chocolate. Ask about any conflicts that may have occurred. Ask how the "Peace Patrol" worked at resolving conflicts. Remind students that conflict happens because we are human. We need God's peace to help us resolve conflicts.

Unit 3

Ultimate Conflict

An unseen force surrounds our kids today. It affects their decisions, self-esteem, and self-worth. Satan works with all his might to undermine the truth expressed in God's Word, and many of our Christian preteens are buying into it. Spiritual Warfare is happening, and we need to prepare our preteens to actively fight the battle! We need to bring truth to the forefront and empower our kids to survive the battles. In doing so, they can make a difference in the world for Jesus!

We are not fighting a battle of the flesh, but one of the Spirit (Ephesians 6:12). The media tells our kids that they must compete with the perfect models pictured in magazine ads, commercials, and TV shows. Kids (and adults) have bought into looks, materialism, and social correctness.

This unit will equip students to enter the battle for their souls and make appropriate choices over Satan's attacks through the power Jesus gives them. In **Session 1** we will expose the big lie that Satan is telling our preteens, through worldly influences (i.e. media, political and social correctness, governmental influences, social standards, and other propaganda). The following sessions will give them the defenses they need to overcome Satan. When Satan whispers, "No one will know" or "Is it really wrong?" preteens need to have a defense. They need to know that God loves them and has provided guidelines to help them grow up to be strong, healthy adults. But Satan's lies

Session 1
Know that God is the supreme authority over all creation, including Satan!
Feel convicted to make God the Lord of their lives!
Pray for every decision they make this week.

Session 2
Know that they stand under the authority of God.
Feel confident that they can stand their ground with Christ under any pressure.
Confront one spiritual issue in their lives.

Session 3
Know that they are forgiven of all sin.
Feel excitement in knowing that they are free from sin.
Tell a family member one thing Jesus has done for them.

Session 4
Know that be hardships occur even after the victory.
Feel they can overcome any hardship through Jesus.
Commit to a daily prayer time.

never stop bombarding our kids. It goes back to the beginning of creation in the Garden of Eden when Satan lied to Adam and Eve by posing the question, "Did God really say that?" He continues to whisper the same lies, and we need to respond with the same truth from God's Word. This is the focus of all the sessions in this unit—discovering and reaffirming God's eternal truth in the face of Satan's lies.

You will be challenged to spend additional time each week praying for your students. Prayer is the key weapon in this raging war. By example, give students a living picture of how prayer changes circumstances and builds character. Boldly tell these kids that you pray for them by name each week. They will not forget the person who diligently brings them before God's throne. It will show them you care.

This unit responds to what the world is throwing at our preteens. They are often much wiser in worldly terms and knowledge than we were at their age. Today's preteens are bombarded by the explosive elements the world hurls at them. Our preteens are hit upon every side, scathed by Satan's schemes, and often left unguarded. Everything in this unit is to be applied to their daily lives at school, at home, at church, and in their world.

Tips for Using These Sessions

1. Memory Verses. Feel free to use a different verse that you feel may be more appropriate for your students. However, hold students accountable to memorize, or at least read aloud, the memory verse for each session. You may want to have students write the memory verse individually on colored strips of paper or colored notecards and tape those to the walls and windows in your classroom during this unit. This will keep the Scriptures in front of your students at all times for reference and reminders.

2. Prayer Time. Each week, encourage your students to spend time in silent or verbal prayer. Ask each student to pray a simple one sentence prayer. You may begin the prayer with a topic of need and have each student say a few words to the Father about the prayer need, then introduce another topic and repeat this pattern. At this age, many kids are self-conscious about praying aloud. This is fine. But as Max Lucado writes in his book *When God Whispers Your Name*, "Better to pray awkwardly than not at all" (p. 143). You may want to challenge the students by telling them you will have group prayer at the end of each session. This will give them some time to build their confidence.

3. Activities. If students participate during the Get Into the

Game section, they will be more likely to participate later in the session. They may even be more willing to pray for a specific need at the end of class.

4. Scriptures. All Scriptures in this unit are from the New International Version (NIV). Look up all the Scripture references before class to feel more confident in helping students understand the text and how it relates to each of them. Again, share how you are affected personally by the Scriptures referenced.

Read the entire lesson first and select the activities that would work best in your class. Also, think about how long it might take for each step. This will give you a better idea of how the session will flow.

Session 1

The Leaders (the commanding officers)

Memory Verse: 1 John 4:4

Know that God is the supreme authority over all creation, including Satan!

Feel convicted to make God the Lord of their lives!

Pray for every decision they make this week.

Get Into the Game

Before this session, cut magazine ads and pictures that show Satan's lies. These will include pictures of pills, alcohol, bad influences, material possessions that "make you accepted by your peers," as well as other valued possessions. Point out that these are the lies Satan would have us believe. He wants us to become so materialistic that we value our possessions more than we value Jesus. Point out that Jesus valued your students so much that He gave up His life for each of them. Satan tries to manipulate while Jesus genuinely cares.

Choose two students to be Leader A and Leader B and have them stand in the front of the class.

Tell Leader A (privately) that whoever chooses to be on his team will receive a sucker, but the other students do not know this yet. Give Leader B a handful of suckers that he can hold, but don't tell him the purpose of these suckers. Do not give Leader A any suckers yet.

Announce to the students that they must choose a leader and stand behind him or her. Then give them an opportunity to choose one of the leaders.

After all students have chosen a leader, have Leader A take the suckers from Leader B and distribute them to those who chose to follow him. Ask the students behind Leader B how they feel about what just happened. (You may get responses such as, "That's not fair," and "We thought . . .") Then read Isaiah 53:2, 3 and 2 Thessalonians 2:8-10.

Ask students to be seated, then say, "You may have thought you would get the reward or prize by choosing the leader with the suckers. But when Satan plays his games, he uses illusions and false fronts to pull you to him, and you will end up with

Materials

bag of suckers or candy, one pair of glasses with no lenses (could be children's plastic glasses), ads from magazines nothing. He offers you what is not his to begin with. Satan gives nothing good."

Show the pictures that you cut from magazines to show how Satan adorns his lies. "Satan may tempt you with the material possession you've always wanted. He offers the perishable, but God offers the eternal. He can break a promise like you can break a wishbone—easily with no hesitation and no guilt. He may appear to be pleasant and full of fun, but he and all who have chosen him will lose. God and all His followers will win! We have a great reward in Heaven. However, we know we have eternal life before we choose Jesus. You didn't know you would receive a reward before you chose Leader A (insert name of student)."

Using a pair of glasses that have no lenses, put them on and say, "We are spiritually blind because we are born into an imperfect world. You and I make choices every day about a number of things. If we don't ask God to help us in every little decision we make, we invite Satan's influence on our decisions. These glasses I am wearing have no lenses because it's up to me to ask God, who is bigger than Satan, to give me spiritual vision to see things as God wants me to see them. If I walk blindly into any decision, no matter how small or big, I will make a decision based upon how I view the situation. In order to benefit himself, Satan will try his best to make choices appealing to me. My prayer for each of you is that when you walk out your bedroom door each day, you will ask God to give you His vision to walk in His path that day."

Take off the glasses and hold them in your hand. Then ask, "What decisions or choices that you may face at school or at home could you ask God to help you with?" Encourage students to think of simple situations they face. You may get responses such as, "Should I try out for the ball team? What should I wear to school? Should I go to my friend's party?" Accept all responses. Say, "Just as real glasses help many of us see objects in perspective, spiritual glasses can help us see things with a godly perspective. When we ask God for guidance on something simple, such as whether or not we should go to a certain event, it helps to remember that it doesn't matter what everybody else is doing. Sometimes Satan may look inviting or attractive because we see him with our human eyes. This is why we have to ask God to help us make every decision with spiritual eyes."

Step 1

Before classtime, attach the two pieces of poster board to the walls. At the top of one poster, write GOD in capital letters. At the top of the other piece, write SATAN. Let the students take turns writing words that either name or describe God and Satan. Some possibilities include:

1. God—Lord, father, almighty, Yahweh, Jehovah, omnipresent, omniscient, omnipotent, creator, ruler of all nations

2. Satan—devil, demon, Lucifer, Beelzebub, tempter, the evil one, fallen angel

If time allows, let the students draw pictures or symbols that could also represent God and Satan. When the students have finished their graffiti posters, have them return to their seats, then ask, "Who is the Prince or the Lord of this world?" Let students discuss this as a group for just a few moments. You may get answers such as "God" or "Jesus" as well as "Satan". Preteens may not have heard Satan referred to as a "prince" or "lord". Then direct them to look up the following Scriptures: John 12:31; John 14:30; 2 Corinthians 4:4; 1 John 5:19.

Have volunteers read each verse. Then have them answer the same question, "Who is the Prince of this world?" Their now-educated responses should be "Satan" or "the Devil." After they answer say, "That's right. Satan is the Prince or Lord of this world. But what does this mean?" Allow time for responses. Then say, "God has given Satan permission to roam the earth (1 Peter 5:8), and Satan can control us if we allow him. God has given us the freedom to choose who we want to follow—God or Satan. Satan cannot have control over you if you choose God. And God will not control you unless you choose Him. When you choose Him, you reap all the benefits of being an heir with Jesus! Wow!"

Direct the students' attention back to their graffiti posters and say, "Let's look at the words you used to describe God and Satan." Alternate reading one word from the God poster and one word from the other poster. Have the students clarify any names or descriptions that may be unfamiliar. Then say, "Keep in mind that God is immeasurably bigger and more powerful than Satan. Satan's army is no challenge for God. But while we are here on the earth, God uses us as His army to combat Satan's attacks. Remember that He will use us and work through us. Our responsibility is to pray and ask Him for the wisdom and power to combat Satan. Satan is bigger than you, but significantly smaller than God! Satan has power. But don't give him too much credit!"

Materials

two large pieces of white poster board, masking tape, colored markers, Bibles

Step 2

Make photocopies of page 104 for this session. Make an overhead of the reproducible, if possible. Look through the statements on the reproducible ahead of time and expound on what they mean.

Distribute photocopies of page 104 and choose one student to read the directions. To carry out this activity, divide students into three or six teams (depending on your class size) and assign one or two of the items per team.

Have students write a response to each underlying message that Satan subtly shoots their way. After students have completed the activity sheet, have them share their answers with the class.

Ask students if they have heard or know what the Yin and Yang symbol means. This symbol seems to have many interpretations. As it is used here, explain to students, "The big lie of Satan may be wrapped up in one of the meanings for the Yin and Yang symbol. The black side represents evil or Satan. The belief is that there is a little good in evil things or in Satan. The white side represents good or God. The belief is that there is a little evil in good things or in God. This is a lie that people have bought into. There is absolutely no shred of bad in God. God is totally Holy. Satan is completely evil. There is no good in Satan. Don't you believe it. Don't even have anything to do with this symbol. You will probably see it around school this year, and the person who wears it probably doesn't know what it means. Satan is happy with the fact that it's being publicized for his purpose whether or not everyone knows its meaning. It is an appealing, popular mix of black and white and looks fashionable—Satan will use that appeal. But remember, God can use anything for His good."

Materials
Bibles, pencils, photocopies of page 104

Step 3

Ask a student to read Ephesians 6:10-13 aloud. Say, "Look in verse 11 and tell me what we are to stand against." Students may read the end of v. 11 saying *the devil's schemes*. Then respond, "Right! This is the Lord's warning for us to watch out for Satan's lies. Satan will lie or scheme to persuade us to follow him by choice, or to follow him by not doing what God says to do, as we have already discussed."

Now say, "Look at verse 12 in your Bibles. What are we struggling against?" If the students have a difficult time answering, have them read the latter part of verse 12—against the rulers, against the authorities, against the powers of this dark world and against the spiritual forces of evil in the heavenly

Materials
Bibles

realms. Then ask, "What does this mean?" You may get responses such as, "We're not fighting against other people, but against spiritual things." Try to get them to verbalize that other men are evil because they have chosen to follow Satan. Then explain, "Many evil things happen in the world, such as abortion and gang violence. Can you think of other evil things that wage war against God's Word?" Include answers such as drugs, rape, cheating, lying, killing, stealing.

Conclude by saying, "These evils are a direct result of Satan's lies and schemes. He lies to people, and they believe his lies. People feel as if they are basically good. If their lives are going OK, then they must be good people. This is Satan's lie. The only way to combat or counterattack him is with the Armor of God! This is not a physical armor, but is a spiritual armor that God gives to help us live the Christian life while Satan shoots his fiery darts (lies and schemes) our way. God's armor covers us from head to toe as we will see next week. You need to leave here committed to reading your Bible every day this week, even if you just read one verse before you go to school."

Take It to the Next Level

Say, "The only way to combat Satan's attacks is to arm ourselves with the armor of Christ. We must be ready at any time to give an answer for the hope that is found within us as 1 Peter 3:15 says. We must put on the armor of Christ. It's not easy. We must actively read the Bible and prepare our hearts and minds. This list of Scriptures will help you be prepared. It's not a once-a-week deal, but a daily commitment."

Materials
Bibles, colored notecards, pens, markers

Have students select one Scripture that best fits their needs from the following list. Have each student write the verse on a notecard, including the reference. Challenge each student to take this home and hang it in an obvious place in his house. Suggest that each time they see this verse, they read it, think about how it applies to their lives, and ask God to give them the grace to apply the verse when they are attacked by Satan.

"Rather, clothe yourselves with the Lord Jesus Christ . . ." (Romans 13:14).

"Therefore, as God's chosen people, holy and dearly loved, clothe yourselves with compassion, kindness, humility, gentleness and patience" (Colossians 3:12).

" . . . Clothe yourselves with humility toward one another, because, God opposes the proud but gives grace to the humble" (1 Peter 5:5).

Say to students, "Next week bring one lie of Satan's that you hear or see happen during the week. We will talk about it and plan a strategy to battle it."

Challenge your students to share prayer needs, as well as praying aloud. This would be a good time to give any personal testimony about your prayer time. Create a sincere, quiet atmosphere for your students to come before the throne.

The Big Lies of Satan

Satan tells us many lies through credible sources. These ideas are often subtle ways to try to get our focus off of God and onto ourselves or Satan. At first glance, nothing may seem to be wrong with some of these statements. Your mission is to find a scriptural defense against such lies. Use the Scriptures to help counterattack the lies Satan tells us. Write a statement for each that will help defuse these lies.

1. "My self-worth is based on what I have."
(John 3:16; Matthew 16:26, 27)

_____
_____
_____
_____
_____

2. "Did God really say that? Is it really wrong?"
(Genesis 2:17; 3:1)

_____
_____
_____
_____
_____

3. "No one will know."
(Luke 12:2, 3)

_____
_____
_____
_____
_____
_____

4. "Only bad people go to Hell. I'm good enough."
(Romans 3:23; 5:8; 6:23; 10:9)

_____
_____
_____
_____
_____

5. "Everybody's doing it!"
(John 3:19-21)

_____
_____
_____
_____

6. "I'll never be good enough for God."
(Romans 5:6-8)

_____
_____
_____
_____

Your Command Post (standing firm in your faith)

Memory Verse: Ephesians 6:13

Know that they stand under the authority of God.

Feel confident that they can stand their ground with Christ under any pressure.

Confront one spiritual issue in their lives.

Get Into the Game

Ask for two volunteers who are relatively the same size to complete this illustration. Have one student stand on a chair and another stand on the floor in front of that chair. Tell the students to grab each other's forearms and begin pulling. The person on the chair should be pulled to the ground fairly easily.

After this demonstration say, "This activity illustrates that it is much easier to be pulled down than to try to pull someone up. This is true in life. Even though you desire to stand firm, Satan will try to pull you down. If you hang around with the wrong crowd or even people who are negative, you may be tempted to follow their patterns. If you think you are strong enough to handle being around non-Christians more than you're around Christians, remember this illustration.

Materials
one chair

Step 1

Have the students read Ephesians 6:13 aloud together. Then ask, "When is the day of evil?" Most answers can be accepted here. You may get answers such as *the evil time before Christ returns* or *any day that Satan works against you.* Then explain, "The day of evil is any time that Satan tries to pull you away from God. This probably will happen in some capacity every day of your lives. All sorts of things can cause a gap between Christ and us and give Satan a foothold. What are some of these things?"

Allow time for students to respond and list their answers on the chalkboard or overhead. Try to include items such as: TV programs, negative commercials, bad language, gossip, holding a grudge, cheating on a test, bad thoughts about someone you don't like.

Materials
Bibles, chalkboard and chalk or overhead transparency and marker, photocopies of page 109, pens or pencils

Then say, "If we are to stand under such pressures, we will need to be prepared and guarded. Let's read on in the same chapter and see how we can do this."

Ask students to keep their Bibles open to Ephesians 6. Distribute photocopies of page 109 and follow the directions.

Step 2

Draw three columns on the chalkboard using the following headings: politics, peer pressure, media.

Materials
Bibles, paper, pens or pencils, chalkboard and chalk

Tell students, "I will divide you into three groups, and I would like you to answer the question, 'How does Satan attack the world in the following areas?' I want you to think of subtle ways as well as obvious ways. Remember last week when I asked you to think of one lie of Satan's that you may have heard or seen during the week and bring it back to class? This would be a good time to write that lie under one of these headings so we can discuss it."

Divide the class into three groups and let them use paper and pencils to brainstorm ideas. Give students three to five minutes to discuss. Then say, "Would one volunteer from each group write your group's responses under the appropriate column." The following is a list of some ideas if your students need help:

1. Politics—wars, scandals, candidates making promises they don't intend to keep, cheating, corruption.

2. Peer pressure—smoking, drinking, lying, cheating, gossiping, disobeying parents.

3. Media—portrayal of bad role models, using sexual images to sell products, watching TV instead of praying or doing devotions.

Read each suggestion aloud and comment on any that need further explanation. Ask the group writing the item to explain why they wrote it. Have students give personal examples.

Step 3

Read Psalm 139:7-10 then say, "David asked a rhetorical question—that is a question with an obvious answer. Where can I go to flee from your presence? We cannot flee or hide from God, but we can make Satan flee from us! This is a great promise God has given to us."

Materials
Bibles

Ask a student to read James 4:7. Then ask, "If we submit ourselves to God and resist the Devil, what will the Devil do?" *(flee)* "Yes, he will flee from us! Let's go back a little bit and read verses 4-7 from the same chapter." After a student has read this say, "Do not choose to be a friend to the world. If you do, you give Satan a foothold and actually become an enemy of God. I know no one here considers himself to be an enemy of God. But God states several times in His Word that if you are not for Him, you are against Him. Let's do as verse 8 says: 'Come near to God, and He will come near to you.'"

Write the letters POW on the board as a visual aid and ask students if anyone knows what a POW is. Then explain, "A POW is a Prisoner of War. It is someone who is captured by the enemy and kept from his allies and friends. If we give Satan a foothold, he can lead us subtly into his path. Actually, Satan can't take us against our will, but if we let him be an influence in our lives, we become easy targets. Satan will take advantage of that in order to pull us into his path of unrighteousness. Satan wants you in his army. He may try to sneak up on you and take you as a POW. He may confront you subtly or obviously. He wants you and will work overtime to get you! But God has already defeated Satan! You must only walk in the grace of God and obey His commandments and He will protect you. You definitely want God watching your back in this spiritual battle."

Ask, "With what weapons has God empowered us?" Have a student read 2 Corinthians 10:3, 4 then comment, "God has given us weapons to demolish strongholds. Let's look at how He has equipped us."

Take It to the Next Level

Ask students, "What are some ways we can be prepared at all times?" You may get answers alluding to the armor of God in Ephesians 6, or comments about praying. Accept all answers that make sense. Then continue, "Let's look at what wisdom the Bible gives us about being prepared."

Have students read 1 Peter 3:15-17. Then ask students how we can be prepared. Say, "I want to challenge you to develop a personal schedule to read the Bible every day and ask God to prepare your hearts for whatever may happen. Also, I want you to jot down one or two items that come up in your prayer time that day." Distribute copies of page 110 and have students fill in the blanks that they can plan for on the paper. Again challenge the students by saying, "Think honestly about what time of the day would work best for you to have a quiet time with God. Are you a morning person? Are you willing to try to be a morning person? Would right after school work best for you? Whatever time you choose, I am challenging you to stick to this schedule for the duration of this unit. I pray that when these sessions are over, this schedule will be a habit for you, and you will continue to read your Bible every day. The hand-

Materials
Bibles, photocopies of page 110, pens or pencils

out shows some suggested readings. You may want to begin with these suggestions and add to them as you go along. If you have any good ideas or topics that work for you this week, bring them back next week and share them with the class. We can learn from each other."

Again challenge your students to share prayer needs as well as praying aloud. As you begin and end the prayer time, ask God to help each student set aside daily time for Bible study and prayer.

Preparing for Battle

Read Ephesians 6:13-18. As you look at this armor, remember we are fighting against the powers of this dark world, not against flesh and blood. Satan uses people as well as things to distract us from our goal. Beside each piece of armor, write what it is called and why we need to put this piece on each day in our quiet time.

What:
Why:

What:
Why:

What:
Why:

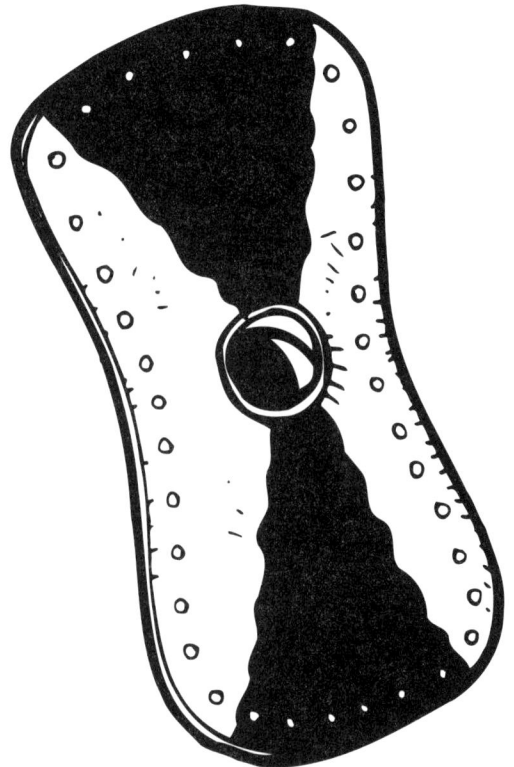

What:
Why:

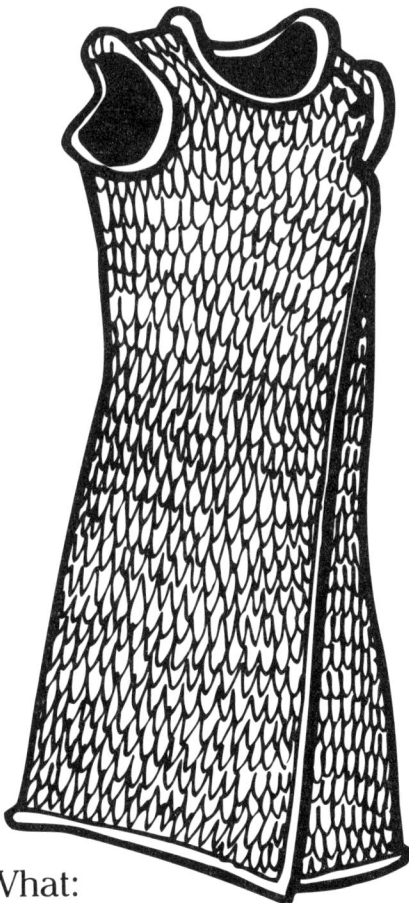

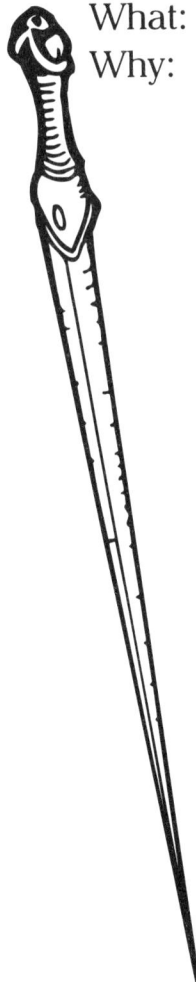

What:
Why:

What:
Why:

Battle Plans

Create a workable daily schedule of Bible reading and prayer.

Suggested Readings:

Ephesians 1:15-23
Ephesians 3
Ephesians 4:17-32
1 John 1
1 John 2
1 John 3
1 John 4
1 John 5

Date	Bible Reading	Prayer Items	Prayer Answers

Session 3

Celebrate the Victory (freedom in Christ)

Memory Verse: Colossians 1:13, 14

Know that they are forgiven of all sin.
Feel excitement in knowing that they are free from sin.
Tell a family member one thing Jesus has done for them.

Get Into the Game

As students arrive, give them a handful of *Play-Doh* or modeling clay. Tell them that in today's session, they will be discussing the concept of victory. They should take the clay and form something that symbolizes victory. Allow five to ten minutes for students to accomplish this. Some possible symbols include: a trophy or an award, a gold medal, a checkered flag, a crown or tiara, flowers, a certificate, a good grade, the cross.

After they have created their symbols, have students show and explain them one at a time.

Then say, "Each of us has experienced some kind of victory. It may have been a good grade on a test, or maybe a sports team we play on won an important game. We've all felt the excitement that comes with winning or achieving. Today we're going to discuss the victory we can experience with Christ in our lives.

Materials
Play-Doh or modeling clay

Step 1

Say to students, "Find Galatians 4 in your Bibles. We will read verses 1 to 7." Take turns reading, allowing students to pass if they don't want to read.

After reading the passage ask students, "What set us free from our slavery?" You should get answers such as *Jesus* or *the cross.* If students don't respond, direct them to verses 4 and 5. Then ask, "Since you are no longer a slave, what does God call you?" Direct students to verses 6 and 7 if they need guidance. "Yes, you are a son or a daughter. God has freed you from your slavery to sin and has adopted you as His children. He will take care of you as your Heavenly father. He will not harm you.

Materials
Bibles

Verse 8 tells us that you are a son and therefore an heir. Do you know what an *heir* is?" Allow time for response. "An heir is someone who will receive all the great riches from the father. What great riches can your Heavenly Father give you?" *(a Christian family, freedom from sin, eternal life, the love of Jesus, redemption, forgiveness).*

Step 2

Distribute photocopies of page 114 and pens or pencils to the class. Have the students quietly read the questions and answer them honestly. Tell the students, "After you finish with these questions, we will use them to act out a talk show."

Materials
photocopies of page 114, pens or pencils

Step 3

Make one photocopy of page 114 and cut the questions apart. Place them in a small basket or bag to draw from. As the teacher, you will act as the talk show host. Begin by saying, "Ladies and Gentlemen, welcome to our first edition of 'Tough Questions.' You, the audience, will help us get to the bottom of these tough questions. Let's begin with this question." Pull one slip of paper and ask the question. Let the students answer. Try to get everyone to join this discussion by saying:

1. Does anyone have something else to add to this discussion?
2. Does anyone in the room disagree?
3. Anyone have a different experience?
4. Why do you think this is true?

Go through all eight questions, allowing discussion on each. Then add, "I am glad you realize that you can overcome anything in your life with Jesus' help. When you live in Christ, He will give you freedom from your sins. You can claim victory in Jesus when you rely on His grace. You will no longer be a slave to sin. We will all fall from time to time. Being a Christian doesn't mean being perfect. However, being a Christian does mean that Jesus will free us from the holds of sin if we trust in Him and give Him control of our lives."

Ask students to open their Bibles to Colossians 1:13, 14 and have the class read this Scripture aloud. Then say, "This is what we can claim victory in. We have been rescued, redeemed and forgiven!"

Materials
one photocopy of page 114 with the questions cut apart, small basket or bag

Take It to the Next Level

Before class, make an overhead transparency of the rap on page 115 and have students recite it together. Make a photocopy for each student to take home.

Materials
photocopies and an overhead transparency of page 115, overhead projector

Say, "Look over this rap." Give the students a minute to do that. Then say, "Look at the overhead. We will recite this rap together." Ask students if anyone would like to lead it. Begin by snapping your fingers to a beat.

After successfully performing the rap, move into a time of prayer by reading, or asking a student to read, John 3:19-21. After the reading say, "Think about the discussion at the beginning of this session. What has Jesus done for you? I challenge you to tell someone in your family, or perhaps a friend, what the Lord has done for you! Let's pray for one another and for ourselves that we may live by the truth and step into the light. Remember that prayer is our number one weapon of resistance and attack against Satan. Let's remember to ask God to lead us into the light and to keep us from falling under the attacks of Satan." Begin the prayer time with praise to God for who He is and ask students to join in as they feel led.

Claim the VICTORY in Christ

Think about how you would honestly answer these questions and write down any thought that might help you state your answers aloud.

1. What attitude has Jesus changed in your life?

2. Have you ever learned a good lesson from a bad experience? Explain.

3. What do you have to be thankful for?

4. When life isn't fair, how do you keep your faith?

5. What does the cross mean to you?

6. Why do you think your parents make rules?

7. Does Jesus care what you do at school? Why or why not.

8. Why is it important to control your thoughts when no one else will ever hear them?

Victory Rap

God is supreme and over all.
Where God is, Satan will fall.
We are His people; God cares for us.
Satan is a liar, so eat our dust!

Jesus is the way, the truth, and life.
He can give us freedom from all our strife.
Satan is the cause of this world's demise.
If he thinks he's gonna win, he's in for a surprise.

If we follow God, we will win.
He's already saved us from our sin.
Satan will try to do his best,
To win our support—but he's failed the test.

If Satan seems to have the victory,
Just sit back in your seat and you will see,
That God has won—it's over now!
All we have to do is take the bow.

It may seem that you're down a lot.
But if you stand you've got your spot,
In Heaven on high, at God's right hand.
You'll be playin' in God's holy band.

Give glory to God in all you do,
And happy you'll be if you follow through.
Remember that God is over all,
And where God is, Satan will fall,

Being a Soldier in God's Army
(dealing with the ambushes after the battle)

Memory Verse: 2 Timothy 2:3, 4

Know that hardships occur even after the victory.
Feel they can overcome any hardship through Jesus.
Commit to a daily prayer time.

Get Into the Game

Before the session, write 2 Timothy 2:3, 4 onto a piece of poster board and display it on a wall in the room. Say, "Let's read this verse together." Have students recite the verse. Then say, "Let's look at some of the pressures a soldier must face."

Make a photocopy of page 120. Cut each section apart and give one slip to each student. If you have more than eight students, make enough copies to have one slip of paper for each student. It is OK to have two or three students with an identical slip of paper. Say, "Look at the first words on your slip of paper written in parentheses. These words are your cue as to when it is your turn to read your section. When you hear someone say the words that are in parentheses, it will be your turn to read. When you hear the cue, stand where you are and read your slip of paper. More than one person may stand at a time, reading the same passage. If this happens, simply read the words in unison." When you have explained how it works say, "Begin."

After the Reader's Theater activity say, "You have just read 2 Corinthians 4:7-9 and 4:16-18. How does this Scripture describe the Christian life?" *(difficult, hard, perplexing, persecuted, troubling)* "Yes, we find that it's not going to be easy. We're promised hardships and persecutions. But let's not forget the rewards—eternal glory. We are told in verse 16 to 'not lose heart'. We may be persecuted on the outside, but what happens inwardly?" Allow time for response. "Yes, we are being renewed! Does anyone know what that means?" Some responses include: *Jesus renews us; Jesus keeps us going; We*

Materials
poster with 2 Timothy 2:3, 4 written on it, photocopy of page 120

get strength every day to keep going. Continue by saying, "Jesus will give us the strength to overcome any hardship or difficult situation that the enemy may put in our way."

Step 1

Ask a student to read 1 Corinthians 10:12, 13 aloud several times. Encourage the students to memorize verse 13.

Materials
Bibles, tag board cut into bookmark-size, markers, colored pencils

Then say, "When you feel you are in a situation where the pressure seems too much for you to handle, remember this verse and say it in your mind. Recalling Scripture is a good way to get you through tough spots. God has given you another promise here. He will not let you face temptation that you cannot handle. This doesn't mean that when you are tempted, you won't ever fall. This means that when you are tempted, God will give you strength and power. If you give in to the temptation, you choose to follow Satan and to ignore God's Word. All you have to do is to ask God to give you the courage to step away from the temptation.

"We need to have perseverance in our Christian lives! We will be tempted, but we can stand if we rely on God to give us perseverance. Perseverance is a trait that Jesus recorded many times in the Bible. What is it, and why is it so important?" Allow time for response. "God has given us a great task. You and I are responsible to tell others about Jesus through our actions and words. If we fall and don't return to Jesus, we lose all those opportunities to tell others about Him. We must stand up under the many attacks Satan will hurl our way. This is perseverance!"

Read 2 Thessalonians 1:3-5. Then say, "These Christians were recognized for their perseverance under trials and persecutions. They suffered and endured for Jesus' name. They were promised a place in Heaven. We, too, have such a responsibility to continue to stand for Christ in the midst of persecutions and sufferings."

Instruct students to take a bookmark and write the word *persevere* along the bottom. They may use colored pencils and markers to decorate the bookmark. Say, "Use the bookmark this week. When you see that word 'persevere,' remember your responsibility as a soldier in God's army."

Give the students a few minutes to create the bookmarks.

Step 2

Materials
Bibles, blank paper

Distribute blank pieces of paper to your class and say, "I am going to ask you to write some very personal information on this paper. No one else will see it. At the end of this session, we will destroy it. Right now, think of one or two temptations you may be facing. Maybe it is something that you've struggled to overcome. Maybe it's something you have never confronted. Think of one thing you would like to overcome and write it on this piece of paper. Then fold the paper and keep it in your hand or Bible for a few minutes." Give the students a few minutes to think about this and write it down.

Have a student look up John 17:15-18 and read it. Then say, "Jesus did not pray for His disciples be be taken out of the world. We need to be in the world to be a Christian influence to those around us. When we are in the world, God promises we will be protected from Satan. Remember that Satan loses in the end; God wins! Don't forget that important promise!

"We have protection through the power of God's Word! Let's look at a few Scriptures that reassure us of this promise." Have students look up the following verses and read them aloud: 2 Corinthians 10:3-6; Romans 16:20; 1 John 5:4; Psalm 32:7; Psalm 91:14; 2 Thessalonians 3:3; John 17:11.

Then say, "John 17:17 says, 'Sanctify them by the truth'. What does the word *sanctify* mean?" Allow time for response. "We are to be 'set apart' or 'made holy' or 'cleansed' before Christ. How are we sanctified before Christ?" Again, allow time for response. "We are sanctified by the truth, and His Word is truth. We can be cleansed through the holy Scriptures. Our responsibility as growing Christians is to be in the Word, to know what the Word says about our lives, and to follow its guidance."

Step 3

This part of the session will be used to review various terminology used throughout the previous sessions. This reproducible will be a way to review terms that compare the Christian life to a soldier's life. Explain the instructions written on the reproducible and give the students about ten minutes to work in small groups or with partners to complete the activity.

The answers are as follows: (1) peace, (2) crush, (3) Satan, (4) weapons, (5) divine, (6) strongholds, (7) captive, (8) obedient, (9) complete, (10) overcomes, (11) faith, (12) suffering, (13) perseverance, (14) character, (15) conquerors, (16) prepared, (17) sanctified, (18) punishment.

Materials
photocopies of page 121, pens or pencils

Take It to the Next Level

Say, "Satan will still attack us as we live the Christian life. We must battle this attack through prayer. We have learned that Satan will attack where we are most vulnerable. He wants to completely destroy our relationship with the Savior.

Materials
a small wooden cross, push pins, hammer, tape or CD player, a recording of "Just As I Am" by Ray Boltz

"This last segment of our study of the armor of Christ brings us to a time of reckoning with Jesus. A little while ago, I asked you to write down an area of temptation that you want to overcome. Get that piece of paper out and consider what you wrote. Think about giving that temptation over to Christ right now. This is a time for you to claim a new start in your walk with the Lord. Take a moment to silently pray about this area in your life and then nail that folded piece of paper to this cross. Make a personal commitment right now to spend time with Him each day in prayer."

Play Ray Boltz's version of "Just As I Am" as the students do this. Allow time for all the students to prayerfully consider their decisions and participate in this symbolic act.

As you move into prayer time, have students join hands and circle the cross. Ask two or three students to pray aloud. Give a few moments for silent prayer. Close by thanking God for His continued protection against the battle with Satan.

Reader's Theater

Cut each section apart and give one slip to each student.

(Begin)
But we have this treasure in jars of clay to show that this all surpassing power is from God and not from us.

(...God and not from us.)
We are hard pressed on every side, but not crushed;

(...not crushed;)
perplexed, but not in despair;

(...not in despair;)
persecuted, but not abandoned;

(...not abandoned;)
struck down, but not destroyed.

(...not destroyed.)
Therefore we do not lose heart. Though outwardly we are wasting away, yet inwardly we are being renewed day by day.

(...day by day.)
For our light and momentary troubles are achieving for us an eternal glory that far outweighs them all.

(...outweighs them all.)
So fix our eyes not on what is seen, but on what is unseen. For what is seen is temporary, but what is unseen is eternal.

Fightin' Words

Look up the Scriptures and find the missing words.
Write them on the corresponding blanks at the bottom.

"The God of (1) will soon (2) (3) under your feet" (Romans 16:20).

"We do not wage war as the world does. The (4) we fight with are not the weapons of the world. On the contrary, they have (5) power to demolish (6). We demolish arguments and every pretension that sets itself up against the knowledge of God, and we take (7) every thought to make it (8) to Christ. And we will be ready to punish every act of disobedience, once your obedience is (9)" (2 Corinthians 10:3-6).

"For everyone born of God (10) the world . . . even our (11)" (1 John 5:4).

"We know that (12) produces (13), perseverance, (14) and character, hope" (Romans 5:3, 4).

"We are more than (15) . . ." (Romans 8:37).

"Always be (16) to give an answer . . ." (1 Peter 3:15)

"A place among those who are (17) by faith in me" (Acts 26:18).

"Then they will go away to eternal (18), but the righteous to eternal life" (Matthew 25:46).

1. _____
2. _____
3. _____
4. _____
5. _____
6. _____
7. _____
8. _____
9. _____

10. _____
11. _____
12. _____
13. _____
14. _____
15. _____
16. _____
17. _____
18. _____

Bridge the Gap

Standing Up for Truth in the Battle of Lies

This session is designed for students and their parents to make family albums that will contain spiritual heirlooms. This is an excellent opportunity for parents to see what their preteens have been studying.

Say to the group, "These past four weeks we have studied spiritual warfare. You are aware of its presence. You know Satan schemes to undermine God's authority. You know your best defense is prayer. And you know if you are in God's army, you will be called upon to fight in the battle. Look around the room and recall the various Scriptures we have discussed over these past several weeks. Today, use what you have learned to create a meaningful scrapbook that displays the Scriptures we have read over the past four sessions and spaces to fill in your family's spiritual ideas. For example, create pages to fill in with the ideas you have about your spiritual battles and goals. You will also have pages for your parents to complete."

Materials
Bibles, markers, glue, glitter, colored construction paper, poster board (white and colored), ribbon, scissors, magazines, yarn, string, stickers, hole punch, pens, other art supplies that are available, photocopies of page 124, pens or pencils, chalk and chalkboard

Distribute photocopies of page 124 and pens or pencils. Allow the parents several minutes to answer the questions. Encourage your students to include pages on prayer. Have them create columns and spaces to keep track of prayers and their answers. Encourage the use of key words and illustrations from the past four sessions as reminders of the spiritual battle (i.e. victory, armor, prayer, freedom, overcome).

Say, "There are several Scriptures written on the chalkboard to get you started. Feel free to use any other Scriptures or ideas you may have." Suggested Scriptures: John 17:15-18; Romans 12:9; 2 Corinthians 4:7-9; 2 Corinthians 4:18; 2 Corinthians 5:7; 2 Timothy 2:3, 4; 1 John 2:28; 1 John 4:4. You may also include any of the Scriptures used in **Sessions 1** through **4**.

Have students punch holes along the sides of the albums and bind together with ribbon, string, or yarn. Encourage students to decorate their albums.

Hopefully the students will enjoy the time they spend with their families on this project. Serve refreshments at the end of the session.

Parent's Response Sheet

1. What spiritual battles have you overcome in your life?

_____
_____

2. What made you choose to follow God instead of Satan?

_____
_____

3. What lessons did you have to learn the hard way?

_____
_____

4. In what ways did you experience peer pressure
and how did you overcome it?

_____
_____

5. What is your greatest victory?

_____
_____

6. When you started to take God seriously,
how did your family and friends respond?

_____
_____

7. Who influenced your life in a spiritual way?

_____
_____

lessons • God • life • spiritual • family • Satan • friends • victory

Go to Extremes

Prayer—The Ultimate Defense

Because prayer is the ultimate weapon we can use against Satan's schemes and manipulating powers, the students will contact others and hold a public prayer session. The prayer time will focus on praying for strength as they fight the spiritual battle for their souls.

The students could participate with their classmates in a morning prayer session, or they could plan and advertise their own prayer time.

The students could plan a prayer time for the church or the community. This could be held at the church building or any public building (courthouse or city hall).

The students could plan a prayer time for the church youth group. This session could be incorporated into a regular youth group meeting.

No matter what type of prayer time the students decide to offer, they need to plan and implement the session. They will need to pick a date and time, advertise, decide what they plan to do at the prayer session, make reminder phone calls, and lead the prayer time.

Advertising is important for the prayer session to succeed. Encourage the students to advertise their prayer session in a variety of ways. The students can advertise to the church body through posters, the church bulletins, and announcements during the services.

To reach the community, they could put an ad in the city or local paper. The students could make small posters to put on community bulletin boards in the grocery stores and libraries. Some poster examples have been supplied on pages 127 and 128. They could design flyers to hand out in neighborhoods or contact a Christian radio station to advertise their prayer session.

Help the students as they plan their prayer session. Encourage them to pray for strength to fight the spiritual battle for their souls. Here are several ideas of what could be included in the prayer time. Use these activities to make suggestions to your students. Mix and match these activities with ones that the students may come up with.

• **Praise time**—Sing several hymns or choruses that are familiar to the people who will attend the prayer session.

• *The Screwtape Letters* **by C. S. Lewis**—Invite a student to explain to whom the letters are written, and read one to the group.

• **"The Champion" by Carmen**—Play this song near the end of the session.

• **Scripture reading**—Invite various students to read these Scriptures throughout the session: 1 Corinthians 10:13; Ephesians 6:10-13; Colossians 1:13, 14; 2 Timothy 2:3, 4; 1 John 4:4. Students could write the Scriptures on index cards and distribute them to people who attend the prayer session. The students could have the Scriptures read at various times during the session.

• **Choose-a-team activity** from **Session 1** (Get Into the Game)

• **Chair activity** from **Session 2** (Get Into the Game)

• **The reproducible** from **Session 3** (page 114)—Distribute photocopies of this page to people as they arrive. Invite them to answer the questions, and then share one answer with someone they do not know.

• **Cross activity** from **Session 4** (Take It to the Next Level)

• **Focused prayer suggestions** from the teaching sessions— Use these sentences at prayer stations set up around the room. Divide the group into three groups and have them rotate from station to station every ten to fifteen minutes.

Pray that you will be clothed with the strength to tell one friend that you are a Christian.

Pray that God will protect you against spiritual attacks.

Pray that you will live in God's light and keep away from Satan's attacks.

SATAN WANTS YOU!

And we're going to talk about it.

when:

where:

sponsored by:

There's POWER in prayer.

Come pray with us.

when:

where:

sponsored by: